READY TO LEARN™

# Summer Workbook

# Ready for Grade 3



## Table of Contents

# READY TO LEARN™
# Summer Workbook
# Ready for Grade 3

## A NOTE TO PARENTS, CAREGIVERS, AND TEACHERS

The Ready to Learn™ series is an excellent tool for assisting your child, grandchild, or student in developing readiness skills in mathematics, reading, and writing during their early learning years. The colorful and engaging workbooks, workpads, and flash cards support the acquisition of foundational skills that all children need to be successful in school and everyday life.

The Ready to Learn™ series develops skills targeted to the Common Core State Standards. The practice workbooks include explanations, strategies, and practice opportunities that engage your young learner with the building blocks needed to become a confident mathematician, reader, and writer. The workpads provide additional practice for the key concepts addressed in the workbooks, and the flash cards support fluency in basic math and reading concepts.

Ready to Learn™ workbooks include a certificate of achievement at the end of each section to present to your child or student upon completion. It is recommended that you display each certificate earned in a prominent location where your child or student can proudly share that he or she is excited to be a learner!

While the Ready to Learn™ series is designed to support your child's or student's acquisition of foundational skills, it is important that you practice these skills beyond the series. You can do this by having your child or student find examples of what he or she has learned in various environments, such as letters and words on menus at a restaurant, numbers at a grocery store, and colors and shapes on the playground.

Thank you for caring about your child's or student's education. Happy learning!

# How to Use This Book

This Ready to Learn™ Summer Workbook was designed to help your child avoid summer slippage and focus on the school year ahead. This workbook includes ten leveled sections that each incorporate Common Core content in reading, writing, math, and science. Levels 1-8 review core grade 2 content and levels 9-10 introduce foundational grade 3 lessons to set your child up for success in the coming year. After mastering each level, kids can tear out a certificate of achievement to reward a job well done. With activities that both strengthen skills learned from the previous year and introduce foundational skills that will be learned in the upcoming school year, this well-rounded workbook will prepare your child for their next academic adventure!

## Skill Sets

Each level in the Ready to Learn™ Summer Workbook series incorporates the following skill sets to help your child review grade 2 and prepare for grade 3.

### Reading and Writing

Phonics
Consonants and vowels
Grammar and punctuation
Sight word practice
Reading comprehension
Foundational writing skills
Graphic organizers

### Math

Counting
Number sense
Pattern identification
Shapes
Addition and subtraction with single and double digits
Multiplication
Fractions
Place value
Time
Money

### Science

Engineering
Chemistry
Experiments

# Level 1 Grade 2 Review

writing

## ABC Order

Putting words into ABC order means they are in the order of the alphabet. Sometimes you need to look at the second or third letter in a word to decide the correct order.

A B C D E F G H I J K L M
N O P Q R S T U V W X Y Z

Put the words below in alphabetical order. You can use the alphabet letters above to help you figure out the correct order for each box.

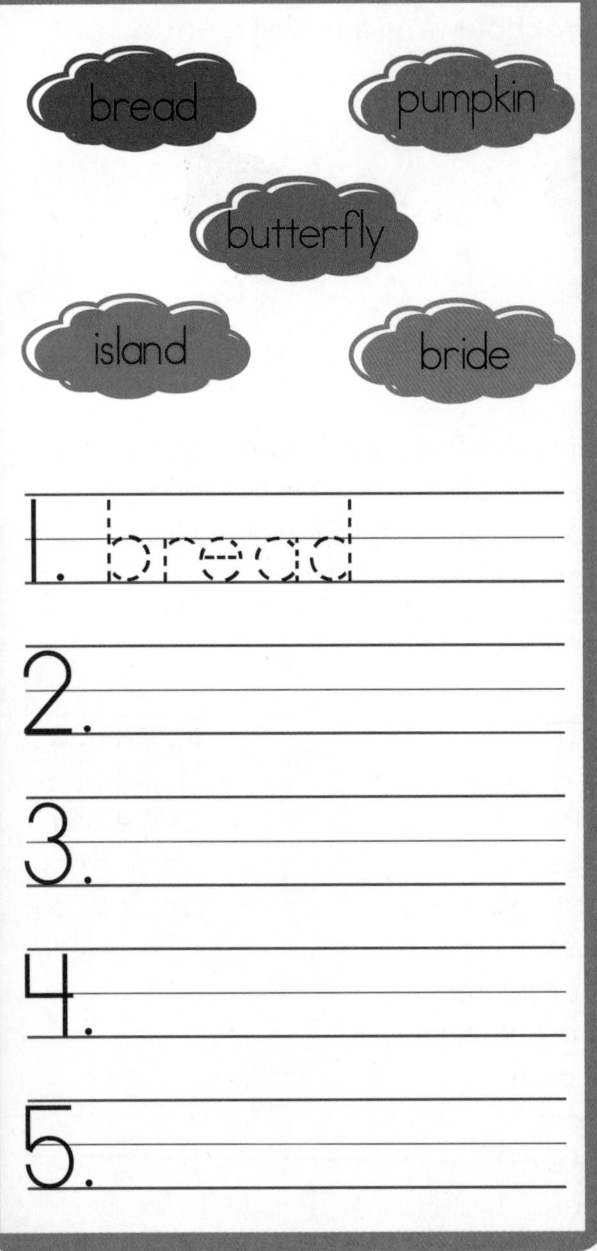

reading

# Phonics

Say the names of the pictures and write the missing letters to complete the words below.

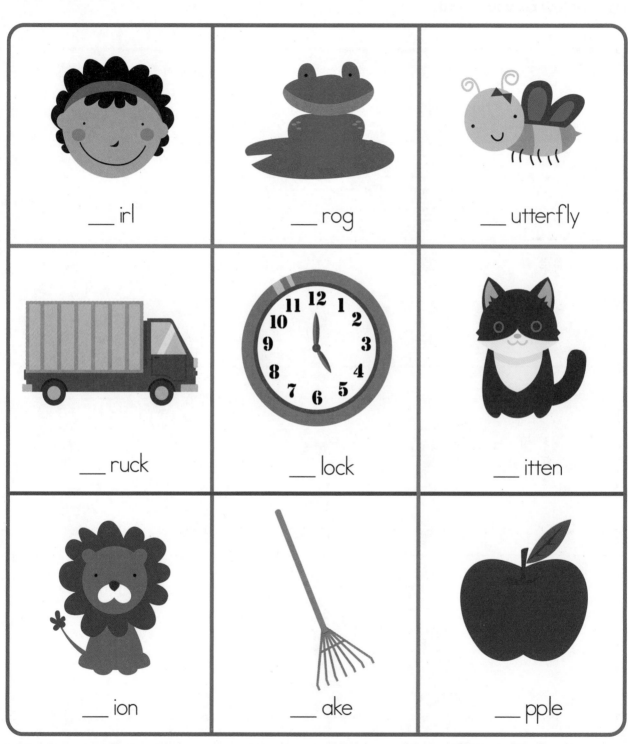

| | | |
|---|---|---|
| __ irl | __ rog | __ utterfly |
| __ ruck | __ lock | __ itten |
| __ ion | __ ake | __ pple |

What two words above start with the same sound but different letters?

123 math

# Number Patterns

Skip counting can make counting faster!

Skip count the flowers by 2s per flowerpot. Write the increasing numbers on the lines below as you count.

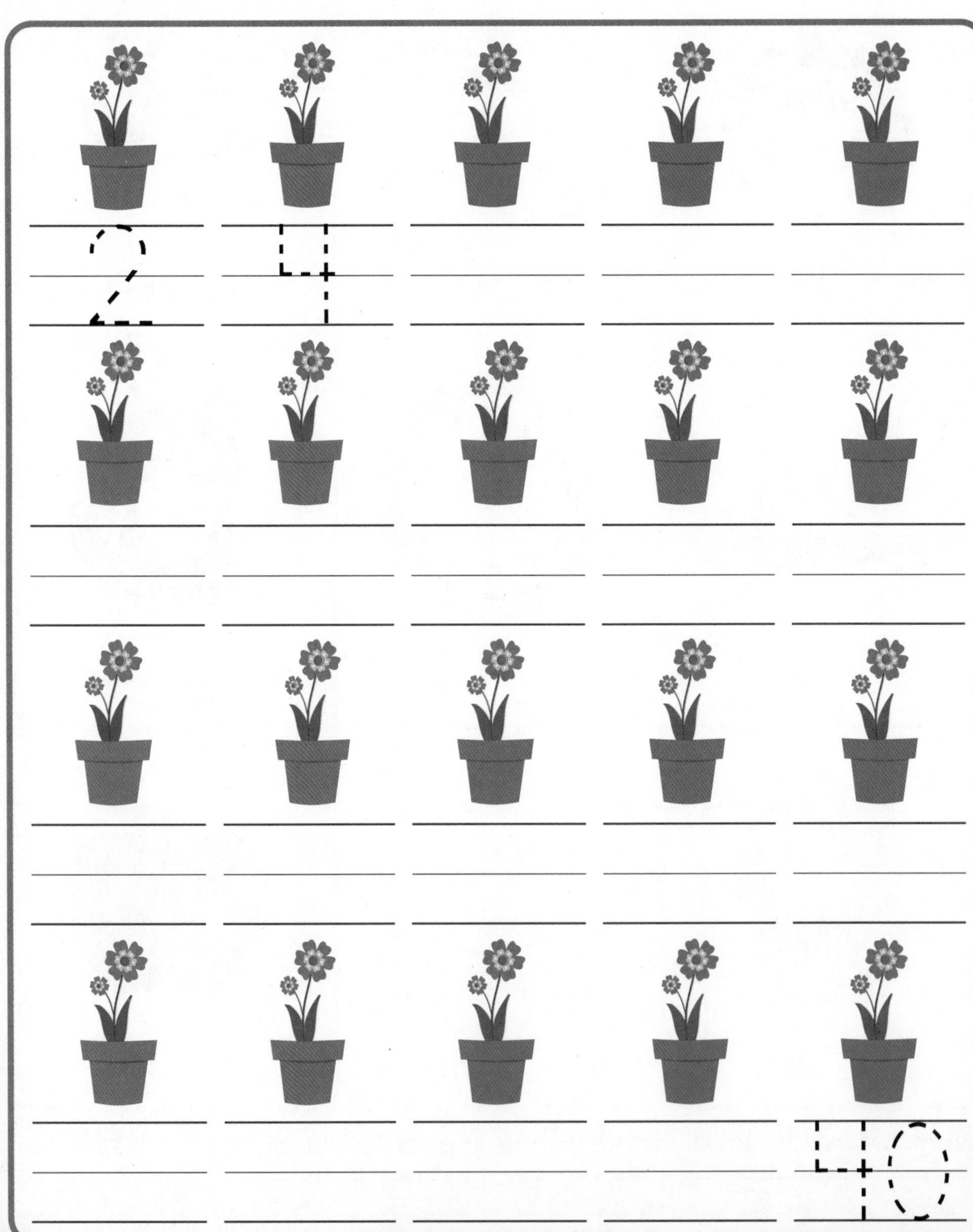

# Consonants and Vowels

Some of the letters of the alphabet are vowels, including a, e, i, o, u, and sometimes y. The rest of the letters in the alphabet are called consonants.

Read the words below and circle the vowels in red and circle the consonants in blue.

carrot

lion

pumpkin

flower

turtle

horse

sea star

shoes

duck

lollipop

frog

octopus

# Phonics

Say the names of the pictures and write the missing letters to complete the words below.

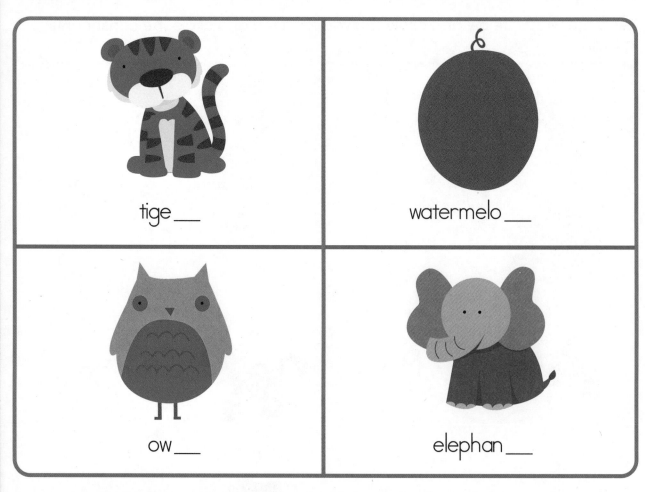

| | |
|---|---|
| tige___ | watermelo___ |
| ow___ | elephan___ |

Draw something in each box that ends with each letter's sound.

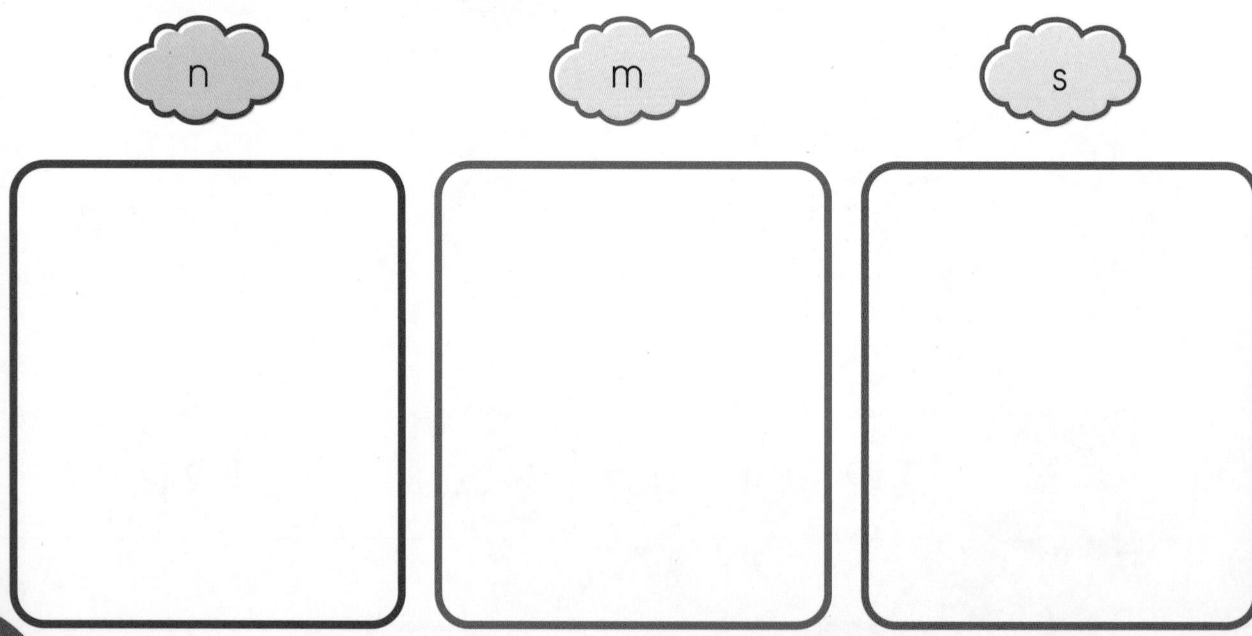

123 math

# Number Patterns

Skip counting by 5s is even faster!

You can count the arms of sea stars quickly because each sea star has five arms. Write the increasing number of arms on each one as you count each sea star by 5s.

# Consonants and Vowels

Vowels most commonly make short vowel sounds, as in dad, jet, gift, fog, and bug.

Vowels can also make long vowel sounds, as in gate, bean, bike, blow, and music.

Look at the pictures and write the missing short or long vowels on the lines below. Say the sounds as you write the letters.

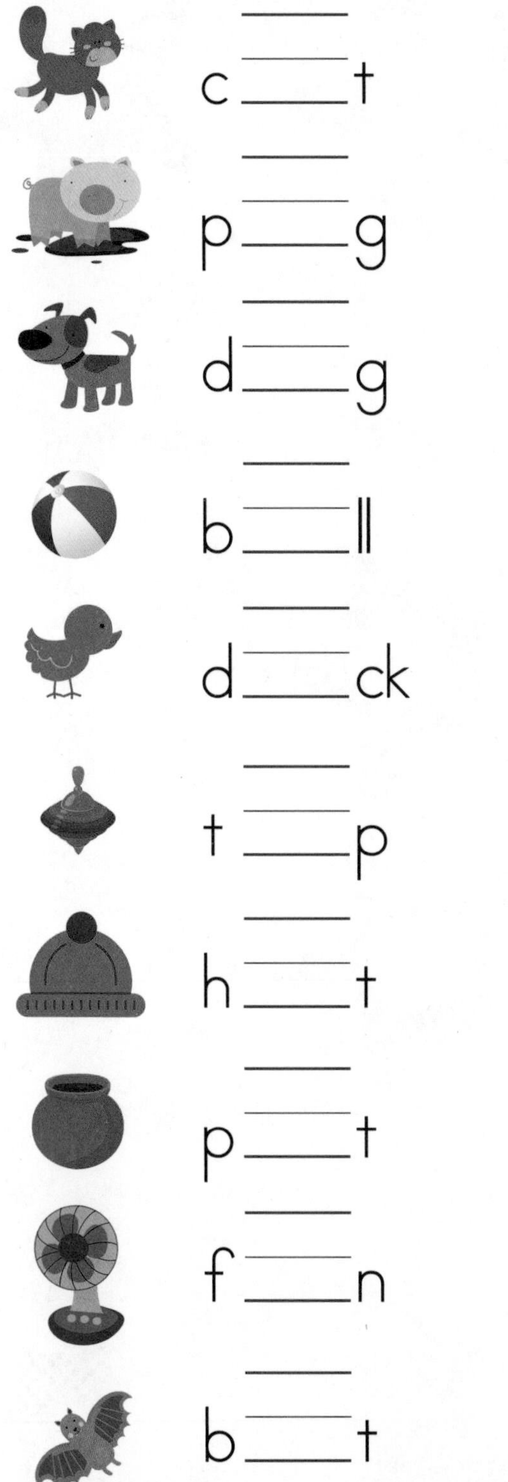


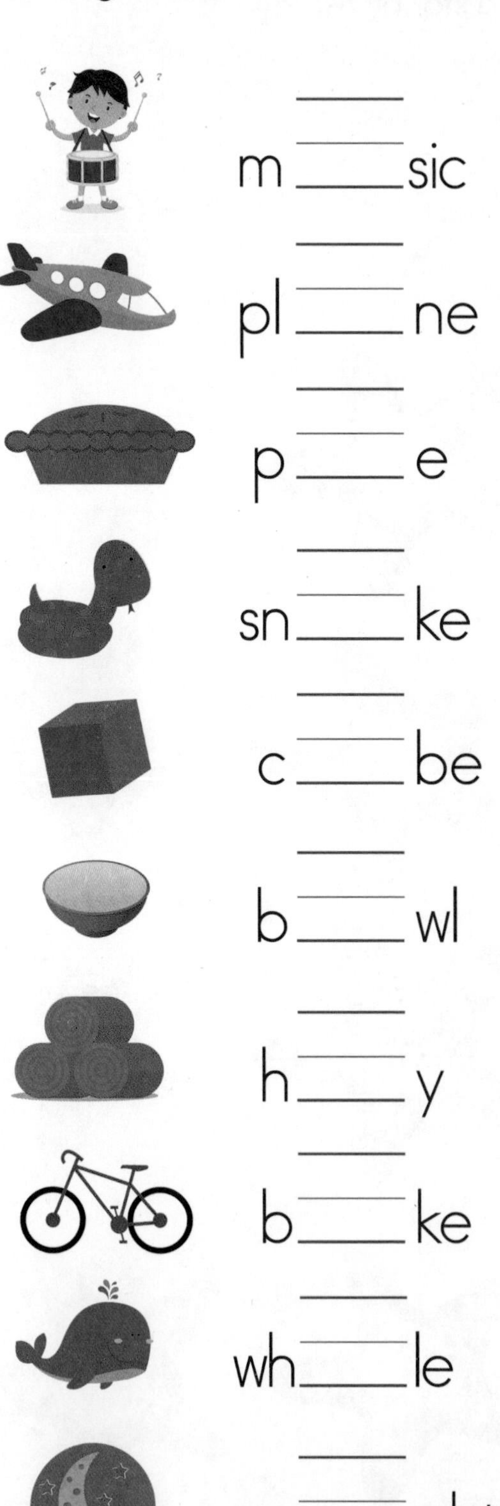

reading

# Phonics

br cr fr gr tr

When you see two consonants together, you blend the sounds.
The blended sounds are called consonant blends.

Say the names of the pictures and listen for the consonant blend sounds.
Write the missing letters on the lines below.

| | |
|---|---|
|  ___ ___ og |  ___ ___ apes |
|  ___ ___ oom | 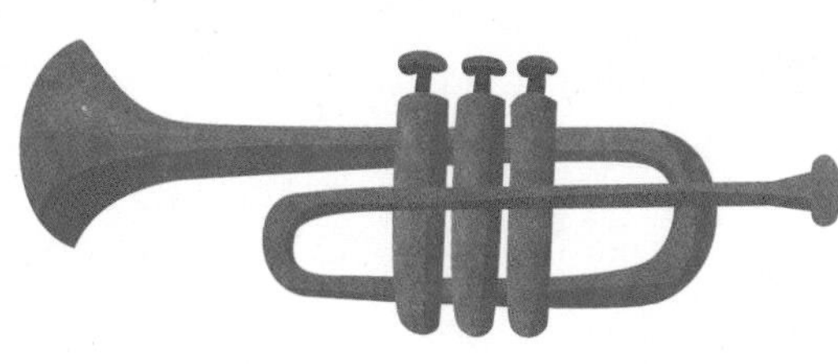 ___ ___ umpet |
|  ___ ___ ab |  ___ ___ een |

123 math

# Number Patterns

Skip counting by 10s is even faster!

Skip count the jelly beans in each jar by 10s. Write the increasing numbers on the lines below as you count.

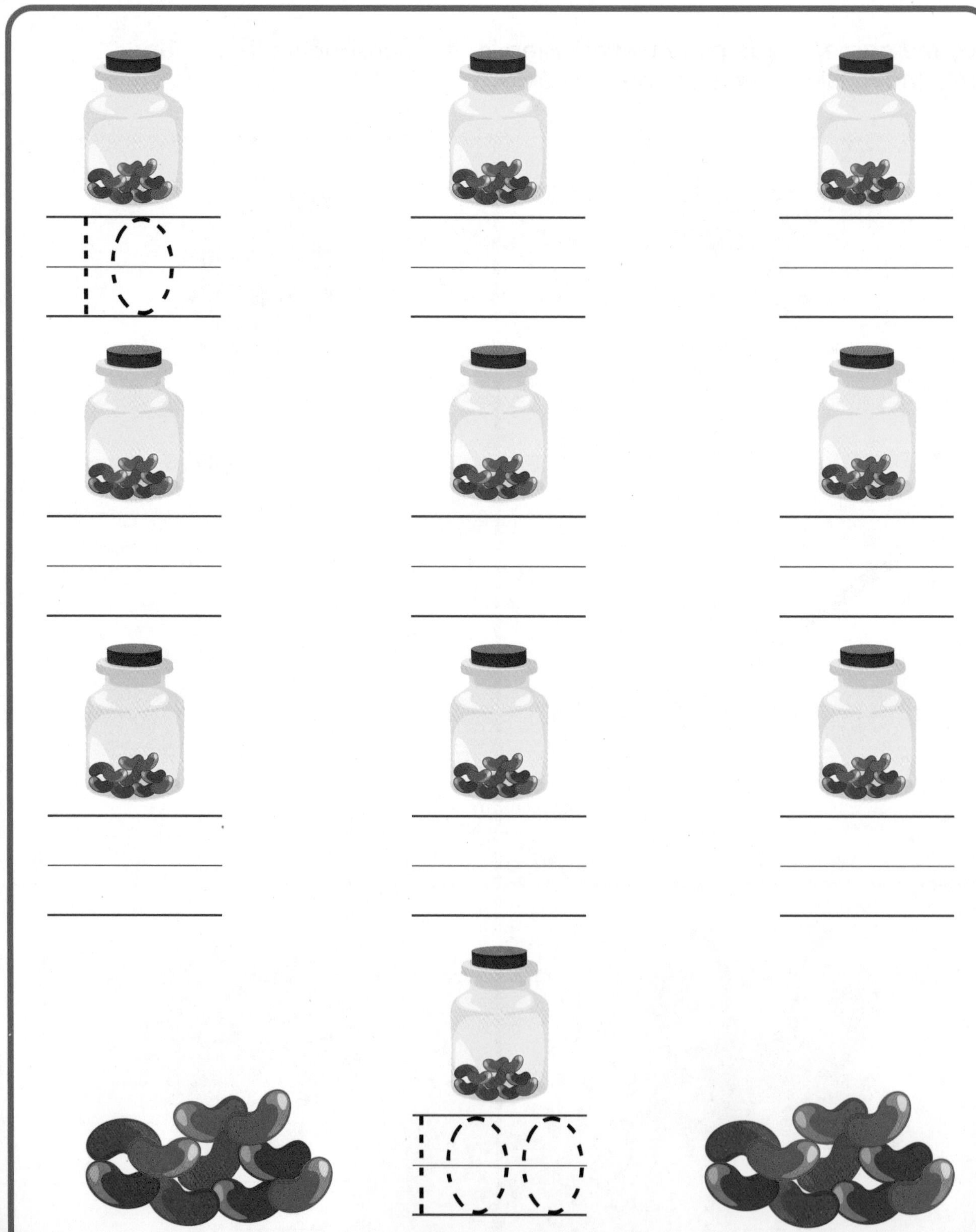

reading

# Consonants and Vowels

**Read the words in the bubbles. Color the short vowel words red and the long vowel words blue.**

reading

# Phonics

bl cl fl pl

**Read the sentences and use the pictures as clues to help you find the missing consonant blends. Write the missing consonant blends on the lines below. Use the list of the beginning consonant blends above to help you.**

The butterfly drinks nectar from a f l ower.

I like to __ __ay with my friends.

My brother builds a tower with __ __ocks.

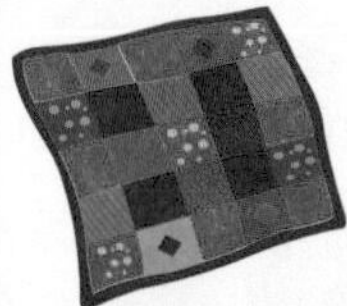

My baby sister likes to carry a __ __anket.

I can tell time on a __ __ock.

I help my mom __ __ean the table.

Earth is the __ __anet we live on.

writing

# Grammar and Punctuation

Look at the sentences below. There is something missing.

Read the sentences and write the proper punctuation at the end. Use a ., ?, or !

I went to the beach with my family __

Yay! We are going to the pool today __

Do you like to eat ice cream __

Look, Mom, my tooth came out __

I can play the piano __

Will you come and play with me __

Write a statement sentence about a pet.

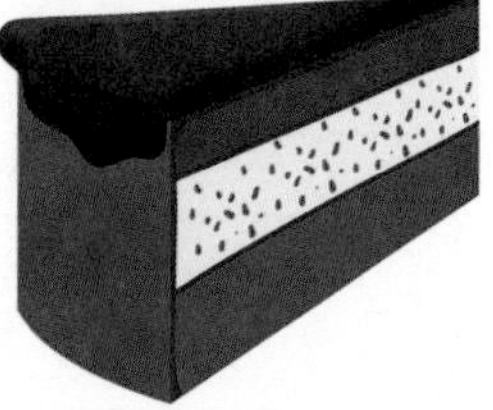

Write a question sentence about dessert.

Write an exclamation sentence about something you are excited about.

science

# STEM Activity

Engineers and architects create plans for new buildings. Skyscrapers need to be strong to support the weight of the building and secure enough to withstand high winds or even earthquakes. Try your hand at building a skyscraper model with items you have from home.

## The Challenge

Build the tallest structure you can in 10 minutes with toothpicks and mini marshmallows.

## Materials You Will Need

- 1 bag of mini marshmallows
- 1 box of toothpicks

## Plan

Explain how you plan to use the materials to build your tower on the lines below.

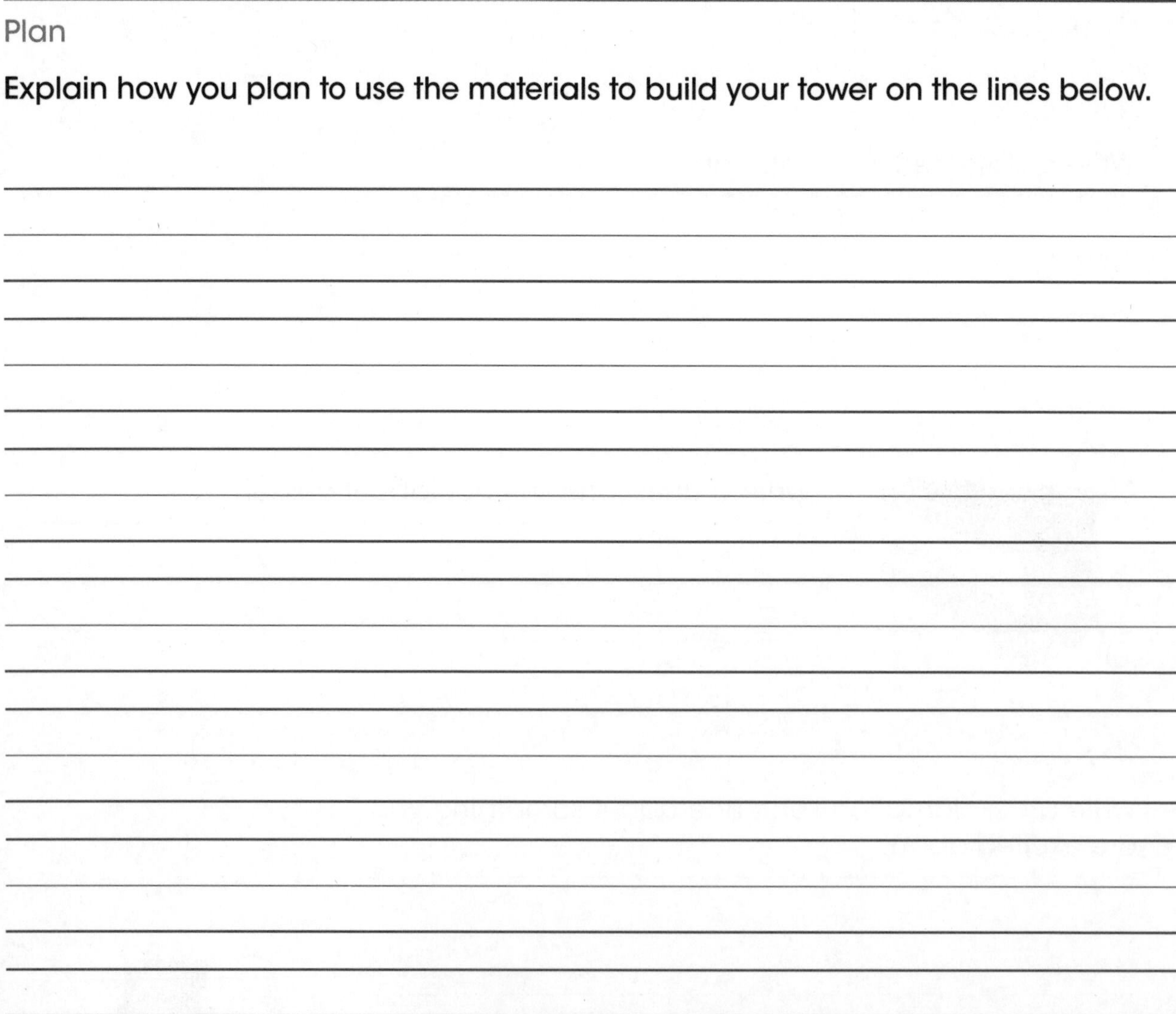

science

# STEM Activity

The Design

**Draw what you imagine the tower will look like in the box below. After that, build the tower.**

# CERTIFICATE
## of Achievement

..........................................

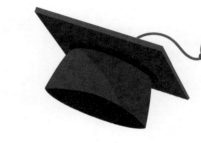

has successfully completed

**LEVEL 1**

Date: ............................

Signed: ............................

# Word Families

Word families are words that all share the same word chunk or letters.

Examples: cat, hat, mat, and flat are all part of the at word family.

Write beginning sounds to create words in each word family below. Try to fill all the lists.

| ock | all | ing | ish |
|---|---|---|---|
| __ock | __all | __ing | __ish |
| __ock | __all | __ing | __ish |
| __ock | __all | __ing | __ish |
| __ock | __all | __ing | __ __ish |
| __ __ock | __ __all | __ __ ing | __ __ __ish |
| __ __ock | __ __all | __ __ing | __ __ __ ish |

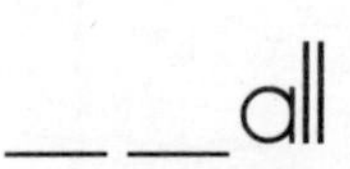

# Phonics

st sn sk sp

Say the names of the pictures and listen for the consonant blend sounds. Write the missing letters on the lines below.

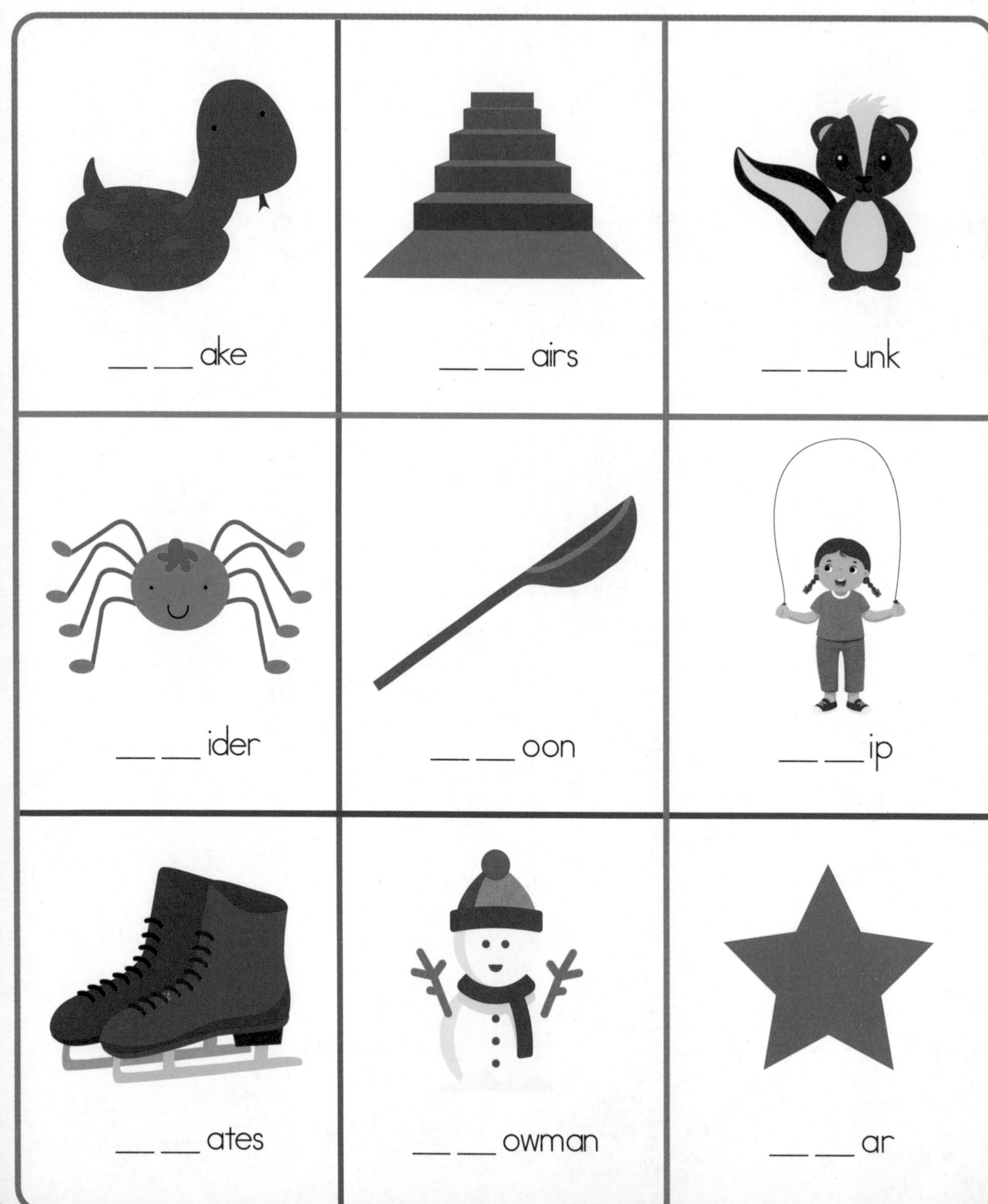

123 math

# Place Value

Look at the illustrations and write the hundreds, tens, and ones on the lines below.

Example:

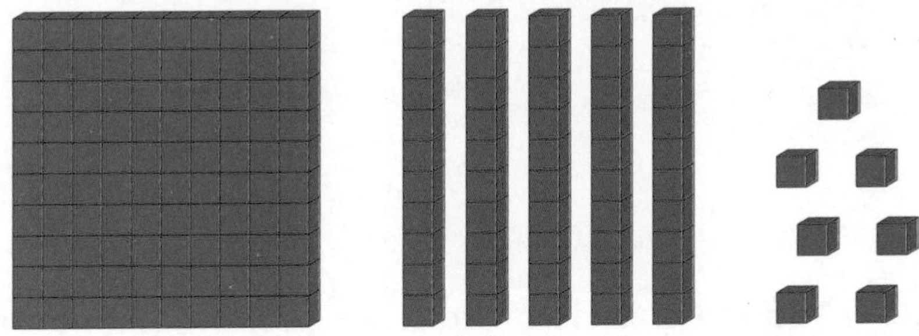

1 hundred **and** 5 tens **and** 7 ones = 157

2 hundreds 2 tens 6 ones = 226

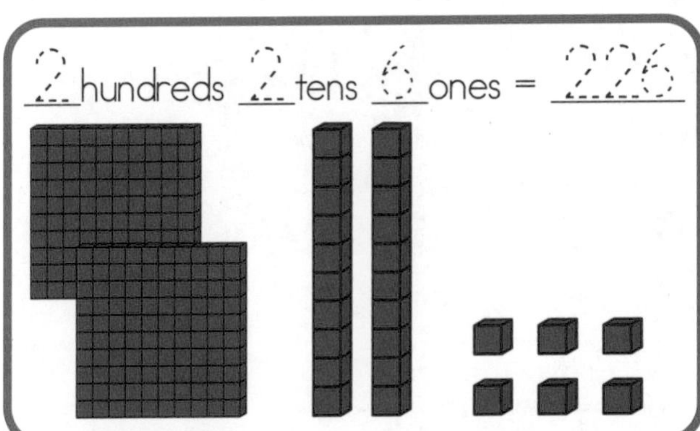

___hundreds ___tens ___ones = ________

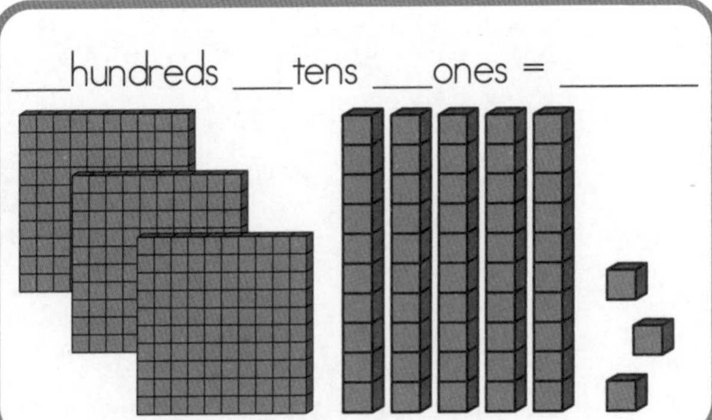

___hundred ___tens ___one = ________

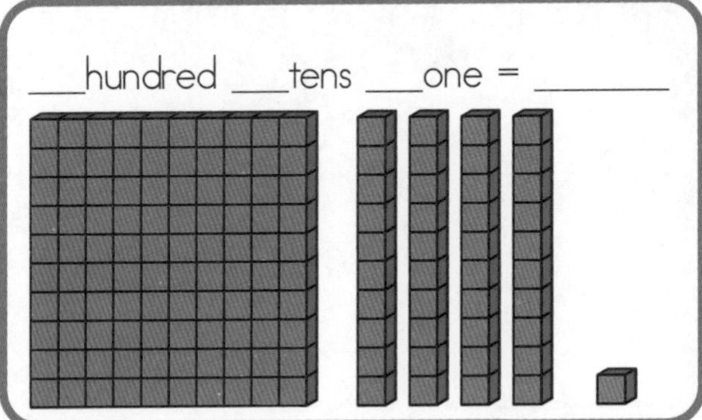

___hundreds ___ten ___ones = ________

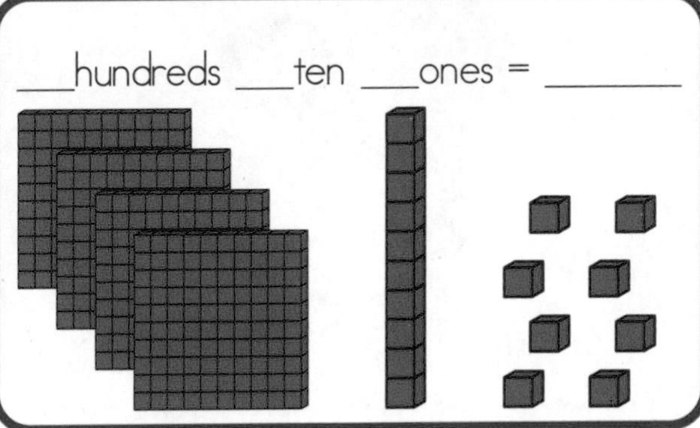

___hundred ___tens ___ones = ________

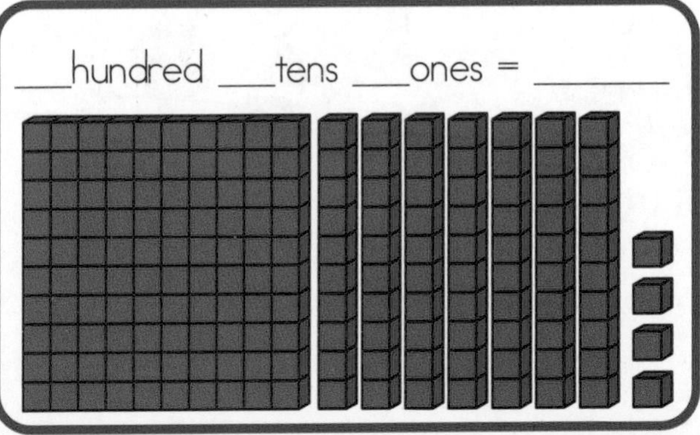

___hundreds ___tens ___ones = ________

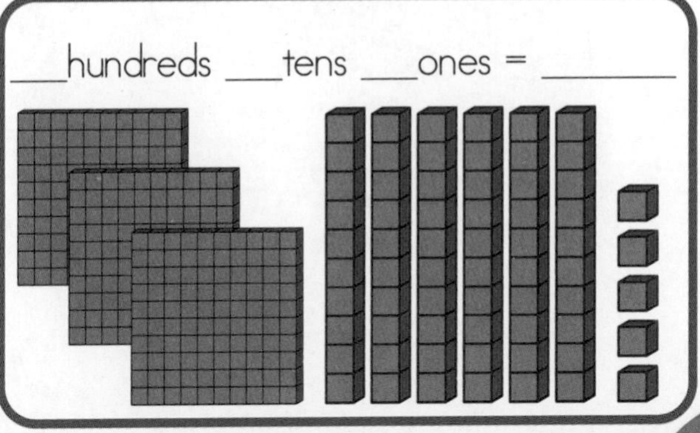

writing

# Prefixes

A prefix attaches to the beginning of a root word to create a new word with a different meaning.

Prefix meanings: un: not, or the opposite of
re: again
pre: before

Example: unhappy means not happy

Read the words below. Add the prefix to make a new word with a new meaning.

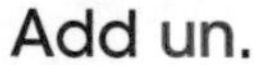

Add un.

____tied ____happy ____locked

Add re.

____turn ____do ____play

Add pre.

_____school _____heat _____view

# Phonics

nt nk mp nd

**Sometimes consonant blends are at the end of a word. Say the names of the pictures and listen for the consonant blends. Write the missing letters on the lines below.**

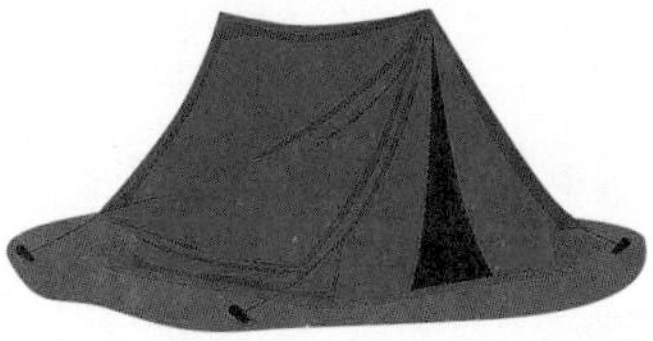

| | | |
|---|---|---|
| te__ __ | pi__ __ | pai__ __ |
| ju__ __ | peppermi__ __ | sta __ __ |
| la__ __ | sa __ __ | ha__ __ |

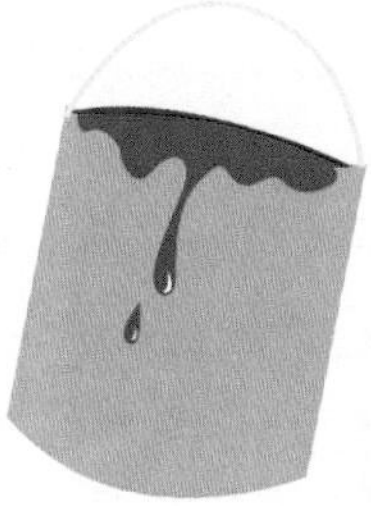

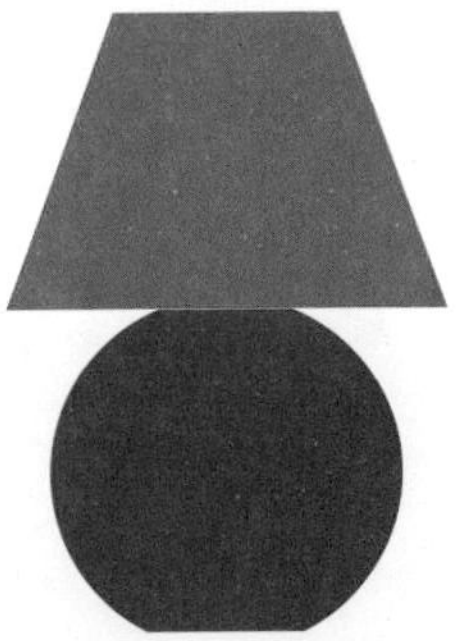

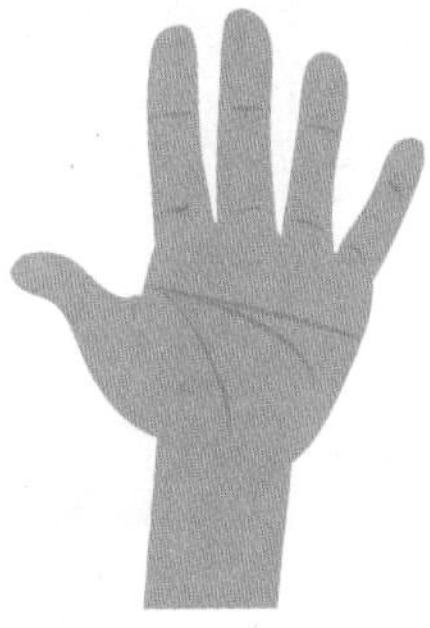

# Place Value

**Read the math stories and answer the questions.**

Libby, a librarian, loves her library books. She has shelves of 100 library books, boxes of 10 books, and single books.

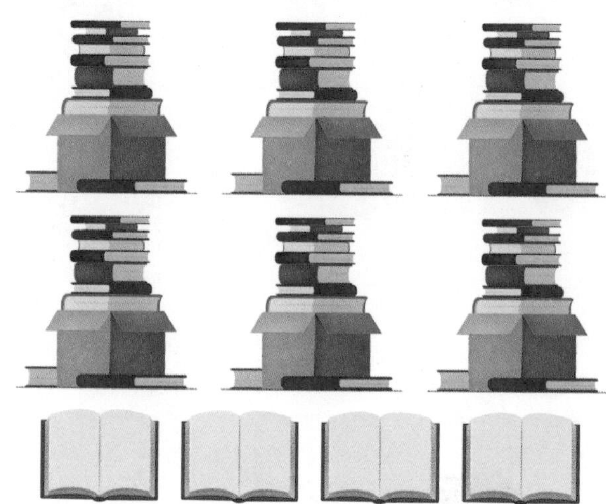

How many books does Libby have? ___________

Ben, a zookeeper, needs to feed the seals! He has crates of 100 fish, buckets of 10 fish, and some single fish.

How many fish does Ben have to feed the seals? ___________

123 math

# Place Value

Expanded form is a way to write a number that expresses the value of each digit. Write the numbers below in expanded form.

Example: 359 = 300 + 50 + 9

| 671 | 283 |
| --- | --- |
| ___ + ___ + ___ | ___ + ___ + ___ |
| 105 | 920 |
| ___ + ___ + ___ | ___ + ___ + ___ |
| 762 | 334 |
| ___ + ___ + ___ | ___ + ___ + ___ |
| 547 | 999 |
| ___ + ___ + ___ | ___ + ___ + ___ |
| 418 | 856 |
| ___ + ___ + ___ | ___ + ___ + ___ |

# Suffixes

A suffix attaches to the end of a root word to create a new word with a different meaning.

Suffix meanings: er: more
est: most

Example: bigger means it is larger than big, and biggest means it is the largest.

Read the words below.

tall dark light short fast

Add the suffixes to make new words with new meanings. Write each word with the first suffix in the first column. Write each word with the second suffix in the second column.

| er | est |
| --- | --- |
| taller | tallest |
| | |
| | |
| | |
| | |

reading

# Phonics

A digraph is a combination of two letters that make one sound. Say the names of the pictures and listen for the digraph sound. Fill in the missing digraphs for each word below.

__ __ ovel

__ __ ocolate

__ __ ine

__ __ irty

__ __ icken

__ __ ip

__ __ under

__ __ ink

__ __ ilis

123 math

# Place Value

Use greater than >, less than <, or equal to = to make the equations true and write the number below each expanded number.

300 + 20 + 1 ( < ) 300 + 60 + 1

321      361

900 + 50 + 3 ( ) 900 + 50 + 1

600 + 0 + 0 ( ) 600 + 10 + 1

200 + 90 + 9 ( ) 200 + 80 + 9

100 + 10 + 1 ( ) 100 + 10 + 1

500 + 30 + 7  500 + 40 + 7

# Synonyms

Synonyms are different words that have the same, or almost the same, meaning.

Example: happy and glad

Draw a line to match each word in the first column to its synonym.

| | |
|---|---|
| fast | begin |
| wet | afraid |
| pretty | quick |
| smart | simple |
| little | tidy |
| scared | beautiful |
| start | too |
| also | small |
| clean | damp |
| easy | clever |

science

# STEM Activity

Engineers and scientists help build the rockets that go to space. Try your hand at building a rocket model with items you have from home.

The Challenge

Build a rocket using materials of your choice. The rocket must be at least 8 inches tall. It must look like a rocket, have wings, and be able to stand up on its own.

Plan

Explain how you plan to use the materials you are using to make your rocket on the lines below.

# STEM Activity

The Design

**Draw what you imagine your rocket will look like in the box. After that, build your rocket.**

# CERTIFICATE
## of Achievement

.......................................................

has successfully completed

**LEVEL 2**

Date: ............................

Signed: ............................

# Antonyms

Antonyms are words that mean the opposite.

Example: happy and sad  

Draw a line to match each word in the first column to its antonym.

| | |
|---|---|
| hot | down |
| front | night |
| day | cold |
| clean | dirty |
| up | back |

Draw two pictures that illustrate two antonym words. Write your antonym word under each picture.

# Phonics

When you see an e at the end of a word, it is usually silent.

The silent e at the end of a word makes the other vowel in the word sound like its letter name. This creates a long vowel sound.

Examples: kite cake bike

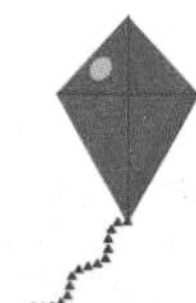

Draw a line from the picture to its matching silent e word.

plane

game

cone

slide

bone

dice

dive

123 math

# Place Value

Put the following numbers in order from greatest to least.

352, 125, 501

501, 352, 125

623, 603, 671

__________, __________, __________

901, 989, 931

__________, __________, __________

232, 721, 43

__________, __________, __________

Put the following numbers in order from least to greatest.

438, 223, 639

223, 438, 639

222, 202, 220

__________, __________, __________

521, 512, 152

__________, __________, __________

726, 861, 672

__________, __________, __________

writing

# Synonyms and Antonyms

A synonym is a word that means the same or close to the same thing as another word. Read each sentence below and circle the synonym of the highlighted word.

| | | | |
|---|---|---|---|
| The towel is wet. | damp | dry | hot |
| The dog is fast. | short | clean | quick |
| The flower is pretty. | hard | beautiful | strong |

An antonym is a word that means the opposite or close to the opposite of another word. Read each sentence below and circle the antonym of the highlighted word.

| | | | |
|---|---|---|---|
| The truck is loud. | slow | red | quiet |
| The boy is short. | smart | tall | sad |
| The snail is slow. | dry | fast | clean |

# Phonics

The letter pairs ai and ay both make the long a sound. When a long a word is spelled with ay, the ay is usually at the end of the word. When a long a word is spelled with ai, the ai is usually in the middle of the word.

Look at the pictures below. Circle the correct spelling of the word.

pail payl

say sai

tail tayl

train trayn

mail mayl

play plai

Read the text. Circle the words that have a long a sound.

Hooray! The rain has gone away.
Now it's time to go out and play.
I will see if Gail can come out today.
It is a perfect sailing day!

# Place Value

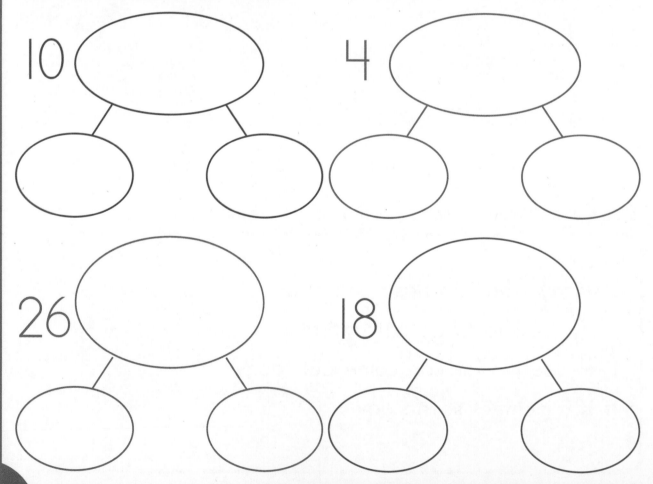

When the digit in the ones place is 0, 2, 4, 6, or 8, the number is an even number. This means the number can be decomposed into two equal groups.

Example:

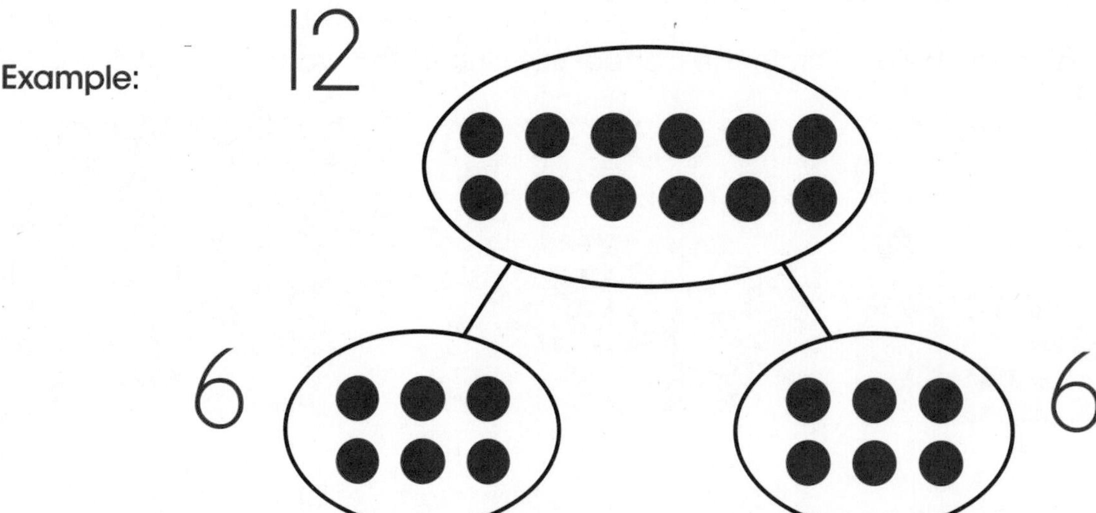


Create equal groups for these numbers. First fill the top oval with the total number of dots. Then divide that number into two equal groups and fill in the bottom two ovals with an equal number of dots.

10

4

26

18

# Place Value

When the digit in the ones place is 1, 3, 5, 7, or 9, the number is an odd number. This means the number will have one left over when decomposed into two equal groups.

Example:

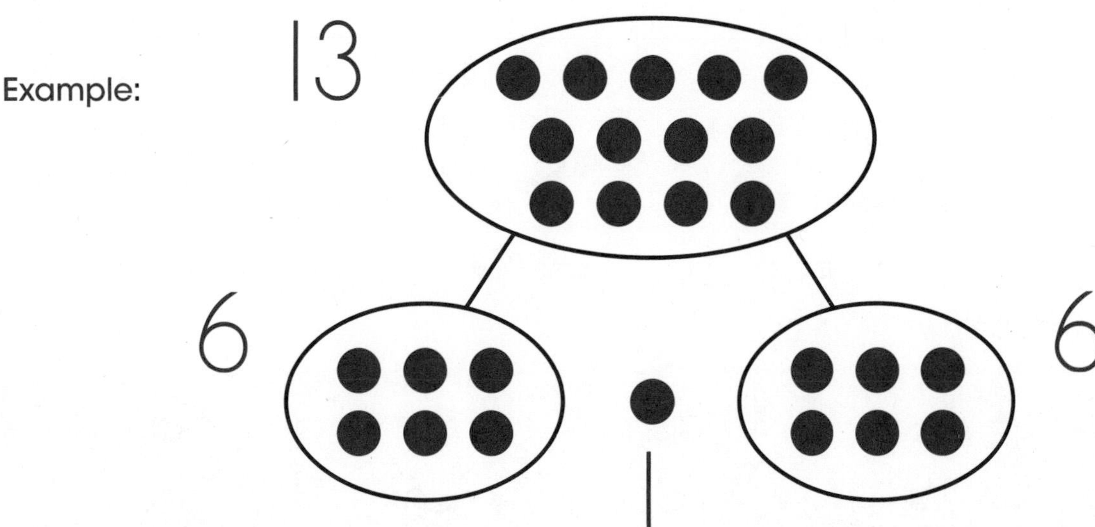


Create equal groups for these numbers. First fill the top oval with the total number of dots. Then divide that number into two equal groups and fill in the bottom two ovals with the correct number of dots. There should be one number left over, so be sure to draw a dot to represent that number between the two bottom ovals.

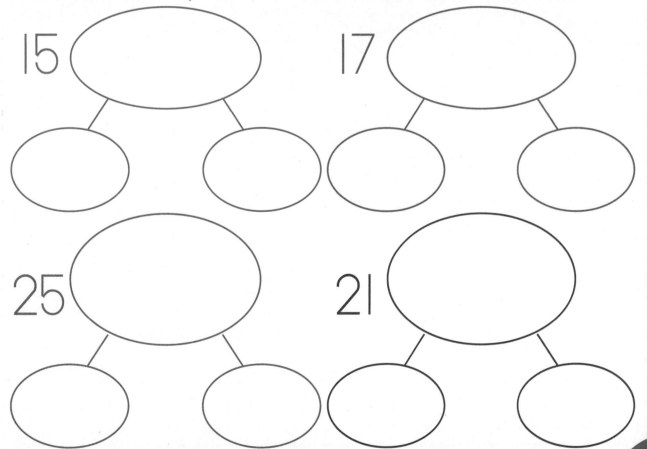

15

17

25

21

writing

# Plural Nouns

Plural means more than one.

To make most nouns plural, you add an s. If the noun ends in ch, sh, s, x, or z, you add es.

Example:

one frog → two frogs    one fox → two foxes

Read the words below.

| dress | kiss | dish | cat | park |
|---|---|---|---|---|
| book | girl | room | lunch | glass |

Write the words with s or es on the lines below in the correct column.

| s | es |
|---|---|
| | |

# Common Nouns

Common nouns are words for people, animals, places, and things.

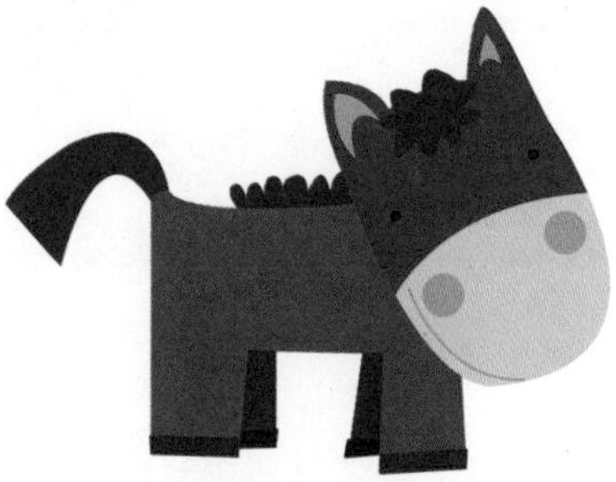

horse

boy

bike

books

shoes

giraffe

Use the nouns from the pictures above to fill in the missing words in the sentences.

A ____________________ has a very long neck.

The ______________ is wearing a blue shirt.

I ride my ______________ to school every day.

I fed a ____________________ at the farm.

I learned how to tie my ____________________ today.

She likes to read her ____________________.

# Phonics

The letters ee and ea both make the long e sound.

Read the sentences below. Choose the correct ee or ea word from the box above to complete each sentence.

My mom asked me to ________________ the table.

My soccer ________________ won the game.

I love green ________________.

My favorite thing to ________ is ice cream.

I ________________ my dog every day.

The king is married to the ________________.

I am wearing shoes on my ________________.

Once, I got stung by a __________.

# Phonics

The letter y at the end of a word sometimes makes the long i sound. The letters igh and ie also make the long i sound.

**Examples:** sky high pie

Read the words and write them in the correct long i sound category below.

| y | igh | ie |
|---|---|---|
| fly | | |
| | | |
| | | |

# Operations

Write double-digit equations below that work for the operation pattern. See the examples below.

Example:

| | |
|---|---|
| even + even = even | 12 + 12 = 24 |
| even + odd = odd | 12 + 13 = 25 |
| odd + odd = even | 13 + 13 = 26 |

even + even = even

26 + 26 = 52

even + odd = odd

+ =

odd + odd = even

+ =

even + even = even

+ =

even + odd = odd

+ =

# Operations

Regrouping **means** changing ones into tens **or** tens back into ones. **Adding two-digit numbers often requires regrouping.**

**Look at the example below.** If the numbers in the ones column add up to more than 9, we need to regroup.

Example: 45 + 19 = ___

First add the ones.

5 + 9 = 14.

14 is more than 9. We need to regroup.

14 means 1 ten and 4 ones.

Put the 4 in the ones column and the 1 at the top of the tens column.

Now add the tens. 10 + 40 + 10 = 60.

Put your tens and ones together. 60 + 4 = 64.

The sum is 64.

| | Tens | Ones |
|---|---|---|
| | 1 | |
| | 4 | 5 |
| + | 1 | 9 |
| | 6 | 4 |

**Solve the equations by regrouping. Write the sums in the boxes below.**

| | Tens | Ones |
|---|---|---|
| | ☐ | |
| | 2 | 6 |
| + | 4 | 7 |
| | | |

| | Tens | Ones |
|---|---|---|
| | ☐ | |
| | 4 | 5 |
| + | 3 | 8 |
| | | |

| | Tens | Ones |
|---|---|---|
| | ☐ | |
| | 2 | 2 |
| + | 3 | 9 |
| | | |

| | Tens | Ones |
|---|---|---|
| | ☐ | |
| | 4 | 7 |
| + | 3 | 6 |
| | | |

| | Tens | Ones |
|---|---|---|
| | ☐ | |
| | 7 | 3 |
| + | 1 | 8 |
| | | |

| | Tens | Ones |
|---|---|---|
| | ☐ | |
| | 4 | 6 |
| + | 2 | 8 |
| | | |

| | Tens | Ones |
|---|---|---|
| | ☐ | |
| | 3 | 6 |
| + | 5 | 5 |
| | | |

| | Tens | Ones |
|---|---|---|
| | ☐ | |
| | 2 | 9 |
| + | 6 | 8 |
| | | |

# Mixing Liquids Experiment

Chemists work with different substances to learn how they interact. Try your hand at mixing some water and vegetable oil to see how they interact together. A liquid is something that flows freely, like water or vegetable oil.

## Predictions

What do you think will happen when we mix water and vegetable oil? Write about what you think will happen on the lines below. Then draw a picture of it in the box.

## Materials You Will Need

- 1 clear cup that you can see through, water, vegetable oil, and a spoon

## Directions

Pour some water in your cup. Fill it less than halfway. Now add about the same amount of vegetable oil. Use the spoon to mix up the water and oil. Now observe what it looks like.

## Observations

What does is look like? Was your prediction right? Draw and write about what you observed.

# CERTIFICATE of Achievement

..........................................

has successfully completed
**LEVEL 3**

Date:  Signed:

............................ ............................

# Common and Proper Nouns

A common noun is a person, place, or thing. Common nouns don't need a capital letter at the beginning of the word. A proper noun is a noun that is the name of something. Proper nouns always have a capital letter at the beginning of the word.

Examples: teacher is a common noun.
Mrs. Everett is a proper noun because it is the teacher's name.

Color the proper nouns purple. Color the common nouns yellow.

Dr. Hayes
Melissa
apple
America
Connor
November
Eric
school
Tuesday
dog
pencil
turtle
teacher
Max
bike
book

# Phonics

The letters oo make two unique long o sounds, like in boot and book.

Examples: boot pool book hook

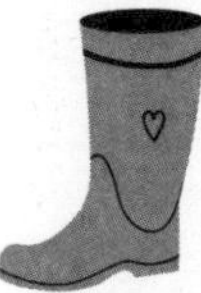

Draw a line from the picture to its long oo sound.

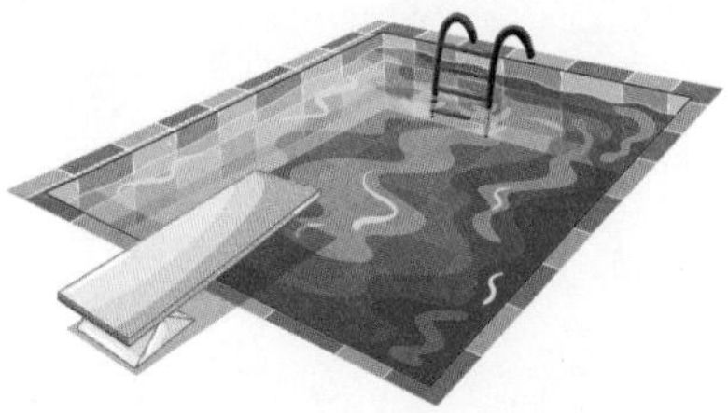

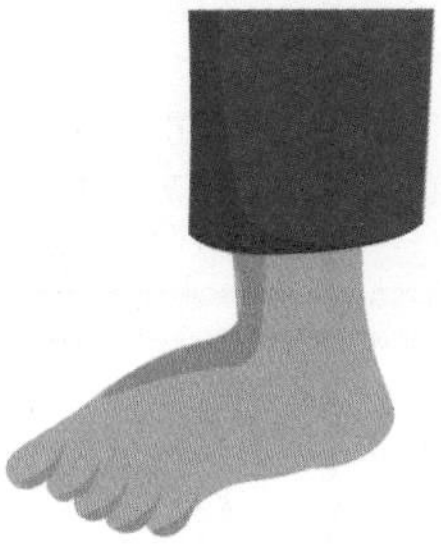

wood

foot

cook

moon

pool

boot

# Phonics

Short vowels do not say their name. For example cat and red. Read the words on the kites below and listen for the vowel sound. Then write the words in the correct short vowel category in the chart below.

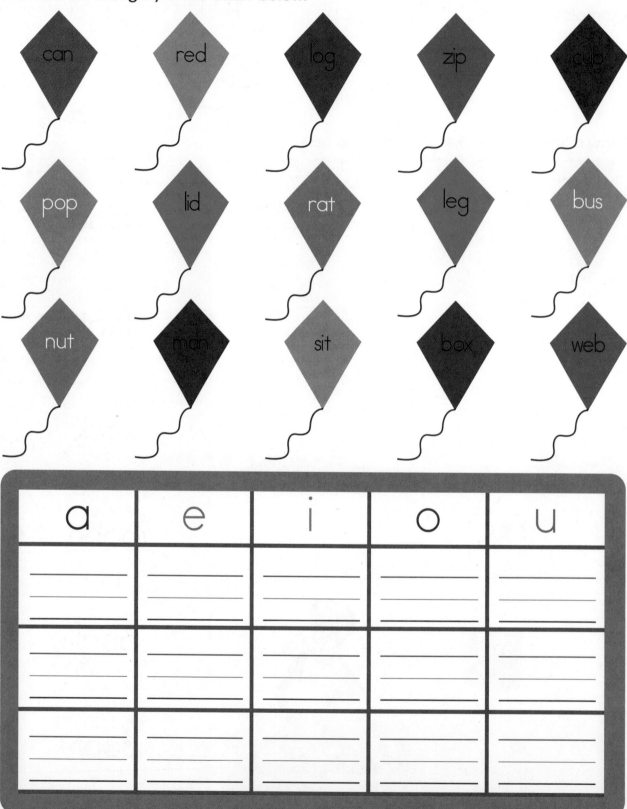

can red log zip cub

pop lid rat leg bus

nut man sit box web

| a | e | i | o | u |
|---|---|---|---|---|
| | | | | |
| | | | | |
| | | | | |

123 math

# Operations

Solve the equations by regrouping. Write the sums in the boxes below.

| | Tens | Ones |
|---|---|---|
| | | |
| | 4 | 9 |
| + | 1 | 8 |
| | | |

| | Tens | Ones |
|---|---|---|
| | | |
| | 2 | 6 |
| + | 1 | 7 |
| | | |

| | Tens | Ones |
|---|---|---|
| | | |
| | 4 | 7 |
| + | 3 | 5 |
| | | |

| | Tens | Ones |
|---|---|---|
| | | |
| | 7 | 4 |
| + | 1 | 7 |
| | | |

| | Tens | Ones |
|---|---|---|
| | | |
| | 1 | 9 |
| + | 2 | 7 |
| | | |

| | Tens | Ones |
|---|---|---|
| | | |
| | 1 | 1 |
| + | 2 | 9 |
| | | |

| | Tens | Ones |
|---|---|---|
| | | |
| | 2 | 3 |
| + | 3 | 7 |
| | | |

| | Tens | Ones |
|---|---|---|
| | | |
| | 4 | 4 |
| + | 1 | 6 |
| | | |

| | Tens | Ones |
|---|---|---|
| | | |
| | 7 | 9 |
| + | 1 | 3 |
| | | |

| | Tens | Ones |
|---|---|---|
| | | |
| | 1 | 5 |
| + | 2 | 7 |
| | | |

| | Tens | Ones |
|---|---|---|
| | | |
| | 5 | 7 |
| + | 3 | 7 |
| | | |

| | Tens | Ones |
|---|---|---|
| | | |
| | 1 | 6 |
| + | 3 | 5 |
| | | |

| | Tens | Ones |
|---|---|---|
| | | |
| | 1 | 5 |
| + | 4 | 6 |
| | | |

| | Tens | Ones |
|---|---|---|
| | | |
| | 1 | 7 |
| + | 2 | 4 |
| | | |

| | Tens | Ones |
|---|---|---|
| | | |
| | 7 | 7 |
| + | 1 | 8 |
| | | |

| | Tens | Ones |
|---|---|---|
| | | |
| | 3 | 9 |
| + | 3 | 5 |
| | | |

# Operations

**When adding three-digit numbers, regrouping is often needed.**

**Look at the example below.** If the numbers in a place value column add up to more than 9 in the ones column or 99 in the tens column, we need to regroup.

**Example:** 545 + 269 = ___

First add the ones.

5 + 9 = 14.

14 is more than 9.

We need to regroup.

14 means 1 ten and 4 ones.

Put the 4 in the ones column and the 1 at the top of the tens column.

| | Hundreds | Tens | Ones |
|---|---|---|---|
| | 1 | 1 | |
| | 5 | 4 | 5 |
| + | 2 | 6 | 9 |
| | 8 | 1 | 4 |

Now add the tens. 10 + 40 + 60 = 110.

110 is more than 99. We need to regroup.

Put a 1 at the bottom of the tens column to represent 10 and a 1 at the top of the hundreds column to represent 100.

Now add the hundreds. 100 + 500 + 200 = 800.

Put your hundreds, tens, and ones together.

800 + 10 + 4 = 814.

The sum is 814.

**Solve the equations by using regrouping. Write the sums in the boxes below.**

| | Hundreds | Tens | Ones |
|---|---|---|---|
| | | | |
| | 7 | 1 | 4 |
| + | 2 | 1 | 7 |
| | | | |

| | Hundreds | Tens | Ones |
|---|---|---|---|
| | | | |
| | 2 | 9 | 5 |
| + | 1 | 2 | 7 |
| | | | |

| | Hundreds | Tens | Ones |
|---|---|---|---|
| | | | |
| | 6 | 3 | 7 |
| + | 2 | 9 | 5 |
| | | | |

writing

# Adjectives

Adjectives are words that describe how things feel, smell, taste, or sound.

**Read the words in each row. Circle the two words that describe each picture.**

| | | | |
|---|---|---|---|
| pink | hot | slippery | dirty |
| fluffy | gray | black | smelly |
| cold | bright | purple | hot |

**Add an adjective that describes the noun in each sentence.**

Kittens are ______________________.

Candy is ______________________.

Rain is ______________________.

Fire is ______________________.

Friends are ______________________.

Dogs are ______________________.

Alligators are ______________________.

# Phonics

**Long vowels say their name, like in go and tape. Short vowels don't say their name, like tub and bar. Read the words in the bubbles. Color the short vowel words red and the long vowel words blue.**

flow
chips
ship
bow
shade
take
hat
feet
crow
apple
cat
snap
peek
show

123 math

# Operations

Solve the equations by using regrouping. Write the sums in the boxes below.

| | Hundreds | Tens | Ones |
|---|---|---|---|
| | | | |
| | 6 | 1 | 5 |
| + | 1 | 9 | 5 |
| | | | |

| | Hundreds | Tens | Ones |
|---|---|---|---|
| | | | |
| | 3 | 4 | 7 |
| + | 4 | 6 | 9 |
| | | | |

| | Hundreds | Tens | Ones |
|---|---|---|---|
| | | | |
| | 2 | 7 | 9 |
| + | 6 | 1 | 9 |
| | | | |

| | Hundreds | Tens | Ones |
|---|---|---|---|
| | | | |
| | 3 | 1 | 3 |
| + | 1 | 9 | 7 |
| | | | |

| | Hundreds | Tens | Ones |
|---|---|---|---|
| | | | |
| | 2 | 2 | 6 |
| + | 4 | 7 | 4 |
| | | | |

| | Hundreds | Tens | Ones |
|---|---|---|---|
| | | | |
| | 1 | 0 | 5 |
| + | 3 | 9 | 9 |
| | | | |

| | Hundreds | Tens | Ones |
|---|---|---|---|
| | | | |
| | 6 | 9 | 5 |
| + | 2 | 2 | 6 |
| | | | |

| | Hundreds | Tens | Ones |
|---|---|---|---|
| | | | |
| | 5 | 8 | 3 |
| + | 1 | 4 | 9 |
| | | | |

| | Hundreds | Tens | Ones |
|---|---|---|---|
| | | | |
| | 4 | 3 | 7 |
| + | 3 | 8 | 9 |
| | | | |

| | Hundreds | Tens | Ones |
|---|---|---|---|
| | | | |
| | 5 | 9 | 4 |
| + | 3 | 7 | 8 |
| | | | |

| | Hundreds | Tens | Ones |
|---|---|---|---|
| | | | |
| | 4 | 8 | 4 |
| + | 3 | 8 | 7 |
| | | | |

| | Hundreds | Tens | Ones |
|---|---|---|---|
| | | | |
| | 6 | 0 | 5 |
| + | 3 | 2 | 7 |
| | | | |

# Adjectives

**Read the sentences below and circle the adjectives in each sentence.**

The brown dog jumped over the big fence.

The marshmallows are soft and chewy.

I got a new summer skirt.

It is hot and dry outside today.

I love my cuddly blue teddy bear.

Look at the shiny gold crown!

# Phonics

The letter c makes two sounds.

It makes a /k/ sound, like in cat.

It also makes an /s/ sound, like in face.
This is what is called a soft sound.

The letter g also makes two sounds.

It makes a /g/ sound, like in goat.

It also makes a /j/ sound, like in giraffe.
This is what is called a soft sound.

When these letters are followed by
y, i, or e, they make soft sounds.

Look at the pictures below. Circle the words that have a soft c or soft g sound.

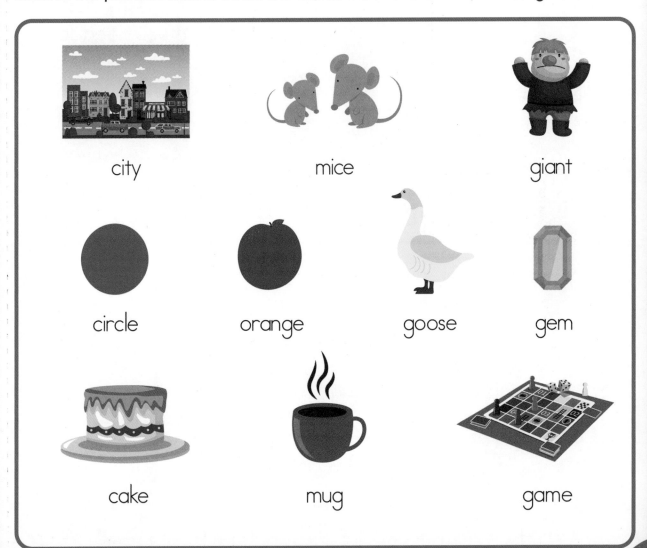

city

mice

giant

circle

orange

goose

gem

cake

mug

game

# Operations

Knowing place value can help you solve addition equations using the column method.

Example:

First add each place value column and keep each sum in the correct column.

| | Hundreds | Tens | Ones |
|---|---|---|---|
| | 2 | 8 | 3 |
| + | 6 | 2 | 9 |
| | 8 | 10 | 12 |
| | 9 | 11 | 2 |
| | | 1 | |
| Now the sum is: | 9 | 1 | 2 |

The 12 in the ones column is 1 ten and 2 ones, so you need to move 1 ten to the tens place.

11 tens means you need to move 1 ten to the hundreds place.

283 + 629 = 912

Solve the equations using the column method.

| | Hundreds | Tens | Ones |
|---|---|---|---|
| | 3 | 6 | 7 |
| + | 2 | 3 | 8 |
| | | | |

_____ + _____ = _____

| | Hundreds | Tens | Ones |
|---|---|---|---|
| | 1 | 2 | 6 |
| + | 4 | 9 | 5 |
| | | | |

_____ + _____ = _____

# Operations

Solve the equations using the column method.

| | Hundreds | Tens | Ones |
|---|---|---|---|
| | 4 | 7 | 2 |
| + | 1 | 4 | 9 |
| | | | |

____ + ____ = ____

| | Hundreds | Tens | Ones |
|---|---|---|---|
| | 1 | 2 | 8 |
| + | 3 | 7 | 5 |
| | | | |

____ + ____ = ____

| | Hundreds | Tens | Ones |
|---|---|---|---|
| | 6 | 7 | 9 |
| + | 2 | 4 | 5 |
| | | | |

____ + ____ = ____

| | Hundreds | Tens | Ones |
|---|---|---|---|
| | 1 | 3 | 8 |
| + | 6 | 2 | 4 |
| | | | |

____ + ____ = ____

# STEM Activity

Engineers create plans for roller coasters. Try your hand at building a roller coaster model with items you have from home.

## The Challenge

Build a marble run roller coaster using materials of your choice. It must look like a small roller coaster and marbles must run from beginning to end without falling off. It also must have a turn, a twist, and a tube.

## Plan

On the lines below, explain how you plan to use the materials you are using to make your marble run roller coaster.

# STEM Activity

The Design

**Draw what you imagine your marble run roller coaster will look like in the box. After that, build your marble run roller coaster.**

# CERTIFICATE
## of Achievement

........................................

has successfully completed

**LEVEL 4**

Date: ..............................

Signed: ..............................

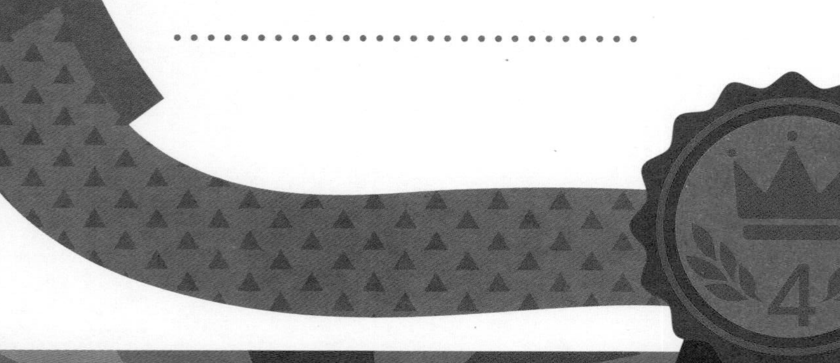

# Verbs

Verbs are words that tell what a noun is doing. They are action words.

drinking

talking

skating

swinging

building

throwing

running

Use the picture above to help you complete the sentences. Write the words on the lines below.

The friends are ______________________ snowballs.

The kids are ______________________ in the snow.

The girl is ______________________ on the swing.

The moms are ______________________ to each other.

The dad is ______________________ coffee.

The boy and girl are ______________________ a snowman.

The people are ______________________ on the ice.

# Couplet Rhymes

**A couplet poem is just two sentences. The sentences end in words that rhyme.**

Example: I found a tiny bug.
It was so cute I gave it a hug.

I enjoy playing in the park.
My dog comes, too, and loves to bark.

**Finish the couplet poems below. Write a second sentence that ends with a word that rhymes with the last word in the first sentence.**

Once, I found a pretty shell.

I have a very happy dog.

I love to ride my big red bike.

I made a wish upon a star.

# Operations

Subtracting tens and ones sometimes requires regrouping.

Look at the example below. If the top number in a place value column is smaller than the bottom number, you need to regroup.

Example: 45 - 18 = ____

First subtract the ones.

5 - 8 = ____

5 is less than 8. We need to regroup.

That means we need to take 1 set of ten from the tens column and move it to the ones column.

Now subtract the ones. 15 - 8 = 7.

Next subtract the remaining tens. 30 - 10 = 20.

Put your tens and ones together. 20 + 7 = 27.

The difference is 27.

| | Tens | Ones |
|---|---|---|
| | 3 | 15 |
| | ~~4~~ | ~~5~~ |
| − | 1 | 8 |
| | 2 | 7 |

Solve the difference equations by regrouping. Write the differences below.

| | Tens | Ones |
|---|---|---|
| | 5 | 2 |
| − | 4 | 6 |
| | | |

| | Tens | Ones |
|---|---|---|
| | 2 | 3 |
| − | 1 | 6 |
| | | |

| | Tens | Ones |
|---|---|---|
| | 4 | 7 |
| − | 2 | 8 |
| | | |

| | Tens | Ones |
|---|---|---|
| | 3 | 3 |
| − | 1 | 9 |
| | | |

| | Tens | Ones |
|---|---|---|
| | 3 | 4 |
| − | 2 | 6 |
| | | |

| | Tens | Ones |
|---|---|---|
| | 4 | 5 |
| − | 2 | 7 |
| | | |

| | Tens | Ones |
|---|---|---|
| | 5 | 6 |
| − | 1 | 9 |
| | | |

| | Tens | Ones |
|---|---|---|
| | 6 | 7 |
| − | 4 | 8 |
| | | |

# Reading Comprehension

Read the story below.

## Hannah's Soccer Game

Hannah was so happy! She had made the starting lineup for her soccer team! It was her third year of playing soccer, and she loved the game. Her favorite position was left fullback. She liked this position because it made her a defender: she had to stop the other team from getting too close to the goal with the ball. She was really excited about the season and liked her team's chances to win this year.

Halfway through the season, she had played in every game and had stopped the other teams from scoring many times. She felt really comfortable playing the defender position and found it very challenging.

It was now the final game of the season. Hannah's team was playing for the championship. It was near the end of the second half with only five minutes to play. It was tied 2-2. Hannah saw her chance and ran hard with the ball. She eyed the goalie on the other team, and she kicked the ball hard into the corner of the net. GOAL!

It was the last goal of the championship, and her team won it all. Hannah felt like a champion because her team got a trophy! Hannah can't wait for the next soccer season to start.

# Reading Comprehension

**Summarizing means explaining the details of the story in just a few words. A story summary should answer these questions: who, what, when, where, and why.**

**Write a few words or a sentence on each line to answer the questions and summarize "Hannah's Soccer Game."**

Who is the main character in the story?

What is happening in the story?

When is it happening?

Where is it happening?

Why did the author write this story? What is the author's purpose?

# Verbs

Read the words below.

Color the winter hats that have verbs on them.

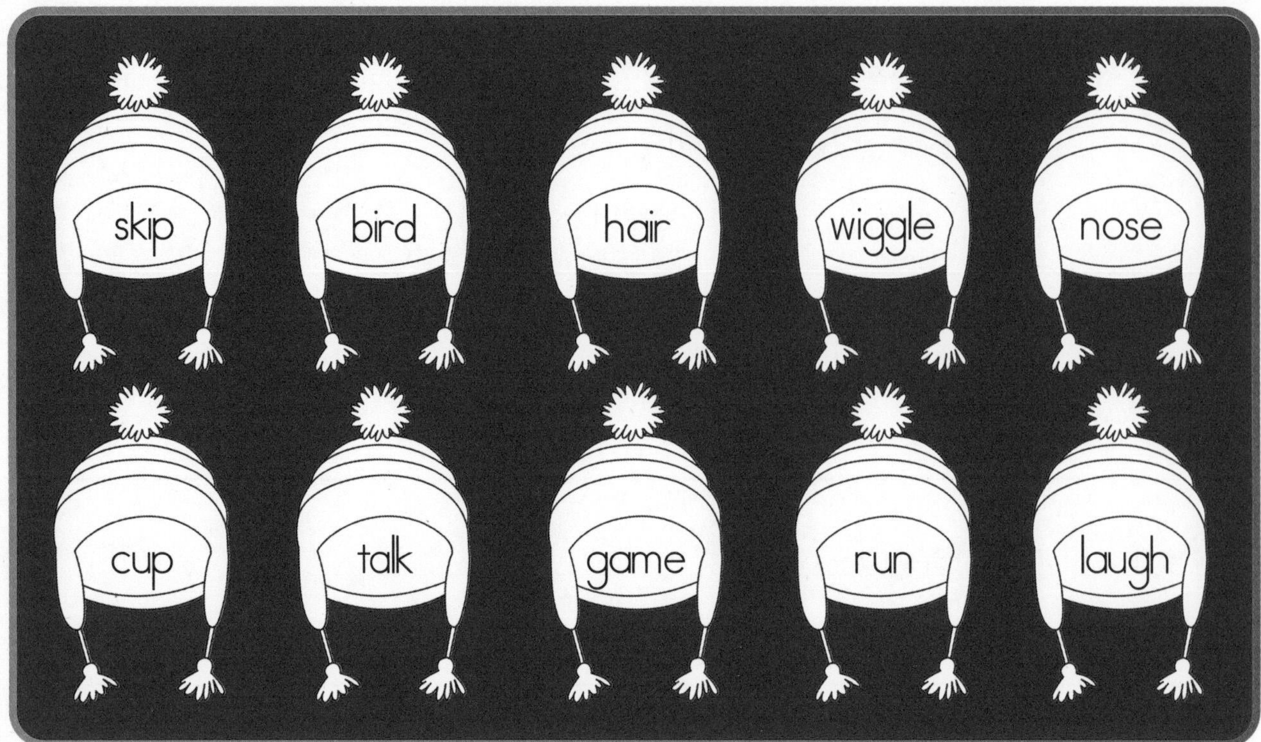


Read the sentences below. Then circle the correct verb to complete each sentence.

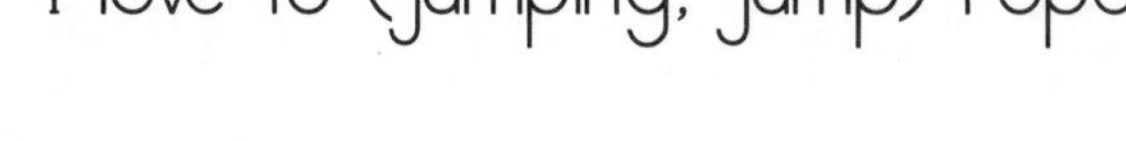
I love to (jumping, jump) rope.

I am (play, playing) a game.

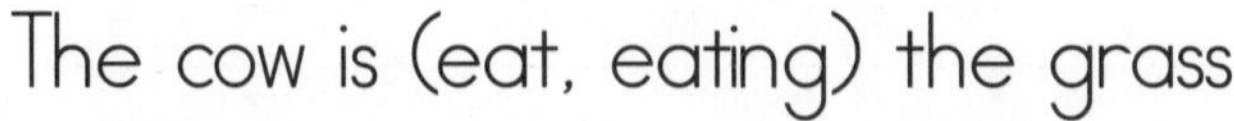
The cow is (eat, eating) the grass.

Can we (go, going) to the playground?

I love (drink, drinking) hot chocolate!

# Operations

Solve the equations by regrouping. Write the differences below.

| | Tens | Ones |
|---|---|---|
| | 3 | 5 |
| − | 1 | 7 |
| | | |

| | Tens | Ones |
|---|---|---|
| | 4 | 7 |
| − | 1 | 8 |
| | | |

| | Tens | Ones |
|---|---|---|
| | 5 | 3 |
| − | 1 | 7 |
| | | |

| | Tens | Ones |
|---|---|---|
| | 3 | 0 |
| − | 1 | 8 |
| | | |

| | Tens | Ones |
|---|---|---|
| | 5 | 2 |
| − | 2 | 8 |
| | | |

| | Tens | Ones |
|---|---|---|
| | 2 | 8 |
| − | 1 | 9 |
| | | |

| | Tens | Ones |
|---|---|---|
| | 4 | 6 |
| − | 3 | 8 |
| | | |

| | Tens | Ones |
|---|---|---|
| | 5 | 4 |
| − | 4 | 7 |
| | | |

| | Tens | Ones |
|---|---|---|
| | 6 | 3 |
| − | 4 | 8 |
| | | |

| | Tens | Ones |
|---|---|---|
| | 7 | 2 |
| − | 5 | 6 |
| | | |

| | Tens | Ones |
|---|---|---|
| | 8 | 7 |
| − | 1 | 9 |
| | | |

| | Tens | Ones |
|---|---|---|
| | 9 | 3 |
| − | 2 | 9 |
| | | |

math

# Operations

**Subtracting hundreds, tens, and ones sometimes requires regrouping.**

**Look at the example below. If the top number in a place value column is smaller than the bottom number, you need to regroup.**

**Example:** 853 - 584 = ____

| | Hundreds | Tens | Ones |
|---|---|---|---|
| | | 14 | |
| | 7 | ~~4~~ | 13 |
| | ~~8~~ | ~~5~~ | ~~3~~ |
| - | 5 | 8 | 4 |
| | 2 | 6 | 9 |

First subtract the ones column.

3 - 4 = ____

3 is less than 4. We need to regroup. That means take 1 set of tens from the tens column and move it to the ones column.

Now subtract the ones column.

13 - 4 = 9.

Next subtract the tens column.

40 - 80 = ____

40 is less than 80. We need to regroup.

That means take 1 set of hundreds from the hundreds column and move it to the tens column. We now have 14 sets of 10.

Now subtract the tens column.

140 - 80 = 60.

Now subtract the hundreds column.

700 - 500 = 200.

Put your hundreds, tens, and ones together.

200 + 60 + 9 = 269.

The difference is 269.

123 math

# Operations

Solve the equations by regrouping. Write the differences below.

| | Hundreds | Tens | Ones |
|---|---|---|---|
| | 6 | 1 | 0 |
| - | 4 | 4 | 7 |
| | | | |

| | Hundreds | Tens | Ones |
|---|---|---|---|
| | 7 | 3 | 1 |
| - | 1 | 8 | 6 |
| | | | |

| | Hundreds | Tens | Ones |
|---|---|---|---|
| | 7 | 5 | 4 |
| - | 1 | 6 | 8 |
| | | | |

| | Hundreds | Tens | Ones |
|---|---|---|---|
| | 6 | 2 | 3 |
| - | 2 | 9 | 5 |
| | | | |

| | Hundreds | Tens | Ones |
|---|---|---|---|
| | 6 | 3 | 3 |
| - | 5 | 6 | 7 |
| | | | |

| | Hundreds | Tens | Ones |
|---|---|---|---|
| | 3 | 7 | 3 |
| - | 2 | 9 | 6 |
| | | | |

| | Hundreds | Tens | Ones |
|---|---|---|---|
| | 9 | 7 | 2 |
| - | 3 | 8 | 3 |
| | | | |

| | Hundreds | Tens | Ones |
|---|---|---|---|
| | 6 | 3 | 2 |
| - | 1 | 8 | 5 |
| | | | |

| | Hundreds | Tens | Ones |
|---|---|---|---|
| | 9 | 8 | 2 |
| - | 3 | 9 | 4 |
| | | | |

# Narrative Fiction

Read the story below.

## Max, the Happy Hawk

Max loved being a hawk! He loved to hunt for food, and he loved to spend time with his friends, Jax and Pax. His life was great, except for one BIG problem: Max was scared of heights!

He loved to fly because he could get from treetop to treetop quickly. He loved to hunt for mice and fish. He even loved to perch up high on a tree limb and look in every direction, except down! He did not like to look down when he was up high. It scared the feathers right off him!

Hawks tend to hunt for their prey from way up high. They fly in large circles, coasting on updrafts of warm air. Max loved doing this. He loved to fly and feel the sun on his back. He could see far into the distance, even if it was a little cloudy. The problem was that when he got hungry he had to look down. His eyes could pick out the furry blur of a tiny mouse down on the ground far below, but when he looked down, he got dizzy and couldn't swoop down to get his dinner. Max's friend Pax suggested he talk to Wise Owl.

Max found Wise Owl and swooped down to perch near him.

"Who, who, whoooo are you?" asked Wise Owl.

"I am Max. I do not like heights, and I get dizzy when I look down!" said Max.

"I think you may need glasses, Max," said Wise Owl.

Wise Owl gave Max a new pair of glasses, and they worked! Max could look down from way up high without getting dizzy. Max REALLY loved flying after that! He didn't get dizzy looking down anymore, and he stopped being afraid of heights. Max was so happy! He was the happiest hawk in the forest!

# Reading Comprehension

Complete the graphic organizer below by writing the main idea and three important events about "Max, the Happy Hawk" in the boxes below.

Main Idea

Important Event

Important Event

Important Event

science

# STEM Activity

Engineers create plans for designing new boats. Try your hand at building a boat with items you have at home.

## The Challenge

Build a boat using materials of your choice. The boat must be at least 6 inches long. It must be able to hold ten pennies and float for 20 seconds. It can have a sail if you choose. Bonus points if you add something to make it move!

## Plan

On the lines below, explain how you plan to use the materials you are using to make your boat.

# STEM Activity

Design

**Draw what you imagine the boat will look like in the box. After that, build your boat.**

# Operations

**Sometimes math equations are hidden in word problems. Read each addition or subtraction word problem carefully and write an equation that shows the unknown number. Solve your equation and write the answer on the line.**

**Example:** Ella makes bracelets for her friends and family. She had 89 but gave some away. She has 56 bracelets left. How many did she give away?

89 - ? = 56  89 - 56 = 33

Ella gave away 33 bracelets.

Oscar collects miniature race cars. He has 29 cars. His friend Caleb has 15 more cars than Oscar. How many cars does Caleb have?

Caleb has _____ cars.

Finn loves the space shuttle. He knows it is 122 feet long and 78 feet wide. How much longer is the space shuttle than it is wide?

The shuttle is _____ feet longer than it is wide.

# CERTIFICATE
## of Achievement

....................................

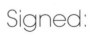

has successfully completed
**LEVEL 5**

Date: ..........................

Signed: ..........................

# Level 6

# Verbs and Adverbs

Adverbs are words that give more information about a verb and can make your writing more interesting.

**Example:** The girl danced beautifully.

Adverbs can answer the questions below.

| How? | How often? | Where? | When? |
|---|---|---|---|
| easily | never | outside | now |
| happily | often | inside | early |
| loudly | seldom | here | after |
| quickly | once | everywhere | before |
| softly | sometimes | home | soon |
| slowly | always | away | today |
| silently | daily | there | since |

Using the list above, add an adverb to each sentence to make it more interesting.

I can tie my shoes ________________.

Do you play the drums ____________?

I can read my book ______________.

They play soccer ________________.

I have dance class ________________.

reading

# Fiction and Nonfiction

A fiction story is a story that is not true.

A nonfiction story is a story that is true. It has facts and information.

Read the stories below and decide whether they are fiction or nonfiction stories. Circle your answer below each story.

## A Field Full of Carrots

Rita Rabbit loved eating carrots. She loved them so much that she ate them all day long. One day, Rita woke up and there were no carrots in the house. She went outside to her garden, and there were no carrots there either! Rita began to get very hungry. She ran and ran all the way to Farmer Frank's field. She found carrots as far as the eye could see. "Thank goodness!" she said. Farmer Frank let Rita bring home two big baskets of carrots to share with her family.

Fiction Nonfiction

## Dinosaurs

Dinosaurs cannot be found on Earth anymore. They are extinct. That means there are no more living dinosaurs. Scientists have researched dinosaurs by digging up fossils and dinosaur bones. They found that some dinosaurs ate meat and some ate plants. There used to be many different kinds of dinosaurs.

Fiction Nonfiction

# Operations

To solve word problems with two steps, you need to figure out what operations you will need to use for each step. You may need to:

add/add — add/subtract

subtract/subtract — subtract/add

**Example:** Molly buys 4 shirts and 5 skirts. She returns 2 skirts the next day. How many pieces of clothing did Molly keep?

First step: 4 shirts + 5 skirts = 9 pieces of clothing

Second step: 9 pieces - 2 skirts = 7 pieces of clothing

Molly kept 7 pieces of clothing.

**Solve the 2-step word problems. Show your thinking by writing the equations and solving for each step.**

There were 20 people on the bus. Then 4 people got off at the next stop. Later, 8 people got on at the last stop. How many people are on the bus when it arrives at the station?

First step: Second step:

Hayley's mom made 26 cupcakes for Hayley's birthday party. Hayley made 10 more. Then Hayley's sister came in and ate 4 cupcakes! Does Hayley have enough cupcakes to serve 30 friends at her party?

First step: Second step:

Circle the answer: Yes, Hayley has enough cupcakes.

No, Hayley does not have enough cupcakes.

# Operations

**Solve the 2-step word problems. Show your thinking by writing the equations and solving for each step.**

There are 18 baseballs and 13 volleyballs in the locker room. There are 10 balls used during practice after school. How many balls are left in the locker room?

First step: Second step:

The pet store has 46 fish in a large tank and 23 fish in a smaller tank. A lady buys 14 fish in the morning. How many fish does the pet store have now?

First step: Second step:

Marcus had 52 markers. He received 12 more as a gift. Then he lost 17 of them at school. Does he have more markers or less markers than he originally had?

First step: Second step:

Circle the answer: Marcus has MORE markers.
Marcus has FEWER markers.

writing

# Compound Words

Compound words are two words put together to make a new word with a new meaning.

Example: paint and brush = paintbrush  

Look at the pictures below and say the words. Put the two words together and write the compound word on the lines below.

 +  = sunflower

 +  =

  +  =

  +  =

 +  =

 +  =

 +  =

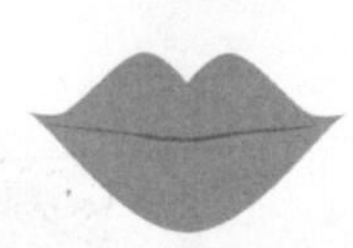 +  =

reading

# Nonfiction

The table of contents tells readers which topics can be found in a book and the pages where they can be found.

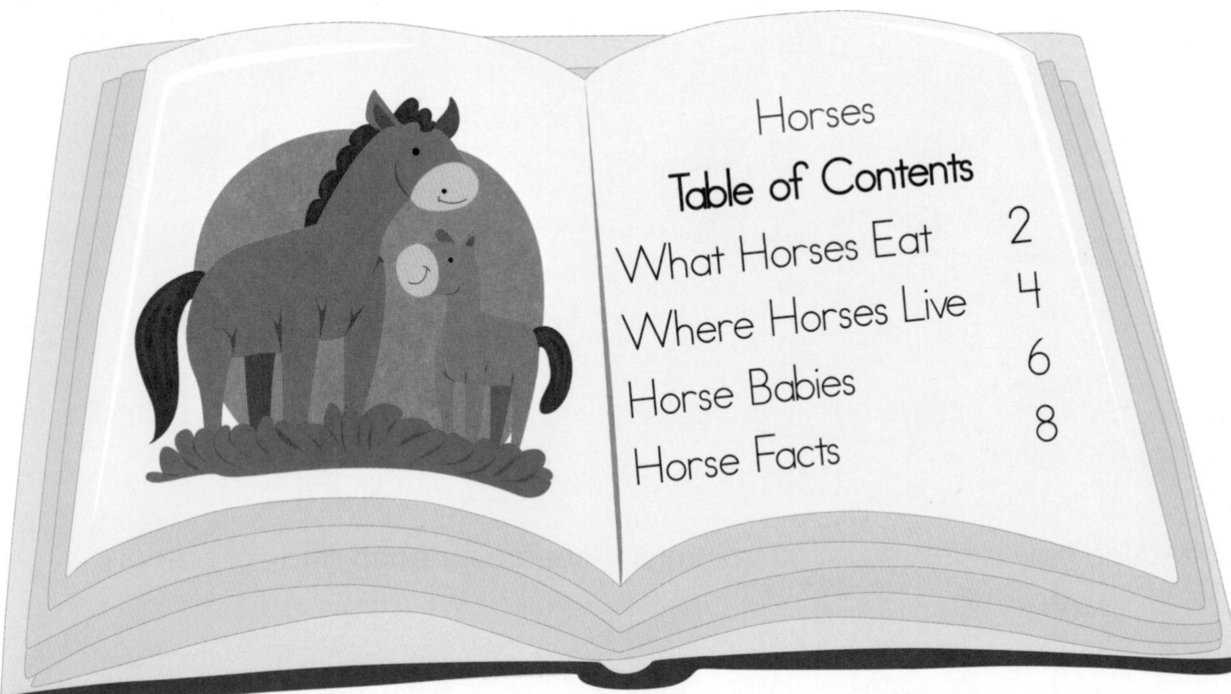


Use the table of contents above to answer the questions. Write your answers on the lines below.

How many topics are in the book?

Which topic begins on page 4?

Which topic begins on page 6?

If I want to find out what horses eat, what topic will help me learn this information?

# Understanding Multiplication

A rectangular array is an arrangement of objects in rows and columns in equal groups. Each row has the same number of objects, and each column has the same number of objects.

Example:

_2_ rows by _4_ columns      _4_ rows by _2_ columns

Both arrays have _8_ circles.

Determine how many rows and columns there are for each array of objects.

____ rows by ____ columns      ____ rows by ____ columns

Both arrays have ____ stars.

____ rows by ____ columns      ____ rows by ____ columns

Both arrays have ____ flowers.

reading

# Nonfiction

Labels give more information to the readers.

Nonfiction books use labels to identify details in the pictures.

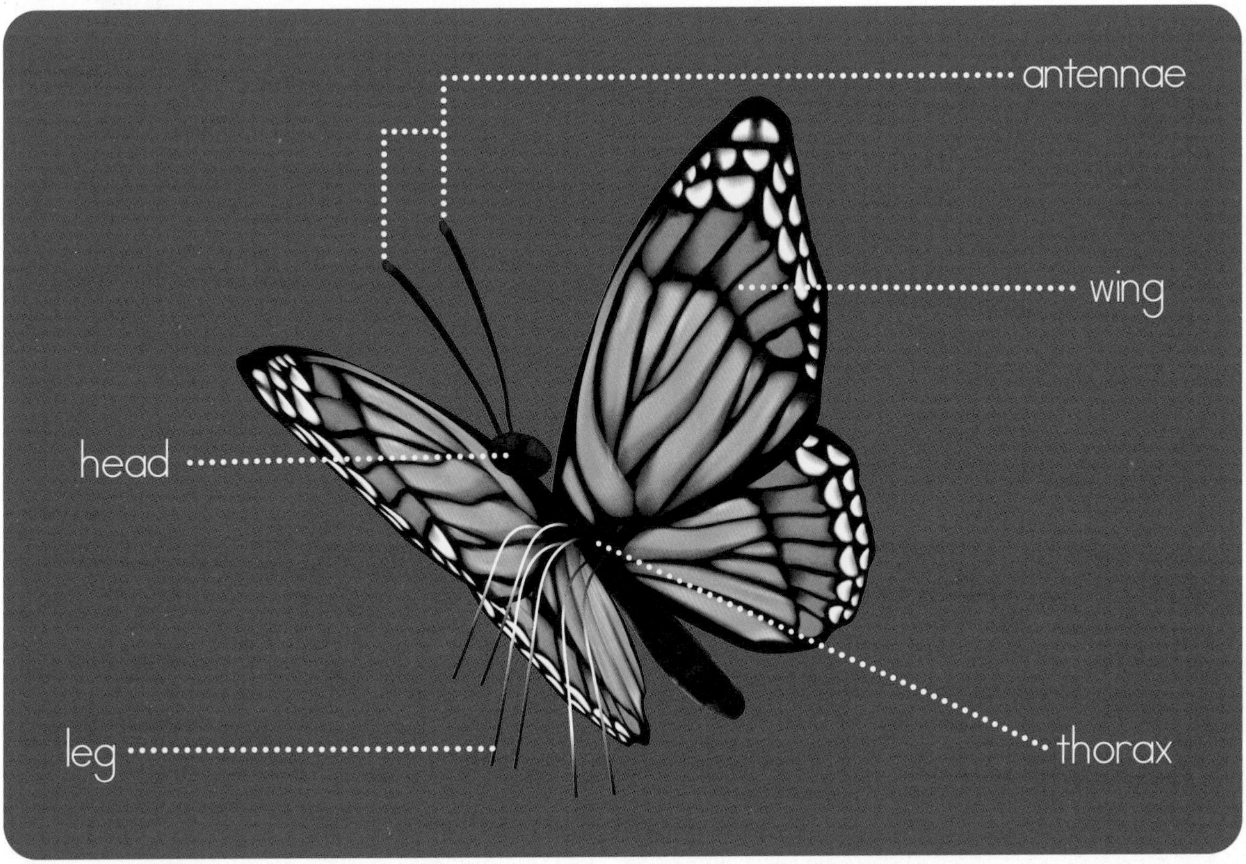

**Use the labeled butterfly diagram to answer the questions. Write your answers on the lines below.**

How many legs does a butterfly have?

______________________________

Are the antennae on the top or bottom of a butterfly's body?

______________________________

What is the head attached to on a butterfly's body?

______________________________

writing

# Contractions

Contractions are two words made into one word. An apostrophe is placed where some of the letters are left out of the new word.

Example: do not = don't

Draw a line from the words to the matching contractions.

| | |
|---|---|
| did not | isn't |
| was not | didn't |
| have not | wasn't |
| is not | haven't |

| | |
|---|---|
| I will | you'll |
| you will | I'll |
| they will | she'll |
| she will | they'll |

| | |
|---|---|
| I am | she's |
| he is | I'm |
| she is | he's |
| it is | it's |

# Understanding Multiplication

You can find out "how many" by combining the same number, or equal groups, of the same number.

Example: 3 groups of 5 is 5 + 5 + 5 = 15 or 3 x 5 = 15

+ + = 15

Solve the equations by combining the groups. Write the numbers on the lines below.

2 groups of 3

3 + 3 = 6

2 x 3 = 6

3 groups of 3

___ + ___ + ___ = ___

___ x 3 = ___

3 groups of 4

___ + ___ + ___ = ___

___ x 4 = ___

4 groups of 5

___ + ___ + ___ + ___ = ___

___ x 5 = ___

2 groups of 5

___ + ___ = ___

___ x 5 = ___

2 groups of 4

___ + ___ = ___

___ x 4 = ___

# Nonfiction

Read the story below.

## Super Shark Facts

Sharks are very interesting and exciting animals. They have been around for millions of years. There were sharks swimming in the ocean long before there were dinosaurs.

There are many different types of sharks. Whale sharks are HUGE! They are the biggest fish in the ocean. They eat tiny crustaceans called krill. Great white sharks are serious eating machines. They eat seals and small whales when they get hungry. They have many rows of teeth and grow new rows of teeth all the time. Great white sharks eat as much as 11 tons of food each year, so they really need all those teeth. Great white sharks are very powerful and can swim almost as fast as cars can go on the highway. One of the reasons great white sharks are such good hunters is their fantastic sense of smell. They can detect blood in the water from nearly 3 miles away! Sharks are awesome!

# Reading Comprehension

Think about the new information you learned from reading the nonfiction story.

Write two things that you learned from "Super Shark Facts" on the lines below.

1.

2.

What questions do you still have?
Write one thing you still want to know about sharks on the lines below.

# Reading Comprehension

A Venn diagram can be used to compare how two or more things are alike and how they are different.

The overlapping parts of a Venn diagram include information about how things are alike. The parts that don't overlap include information about how things are different.

Think about two different kinds of sharks from "Super Shark Facts" and write how they are alike and different in the Venn diagram below.

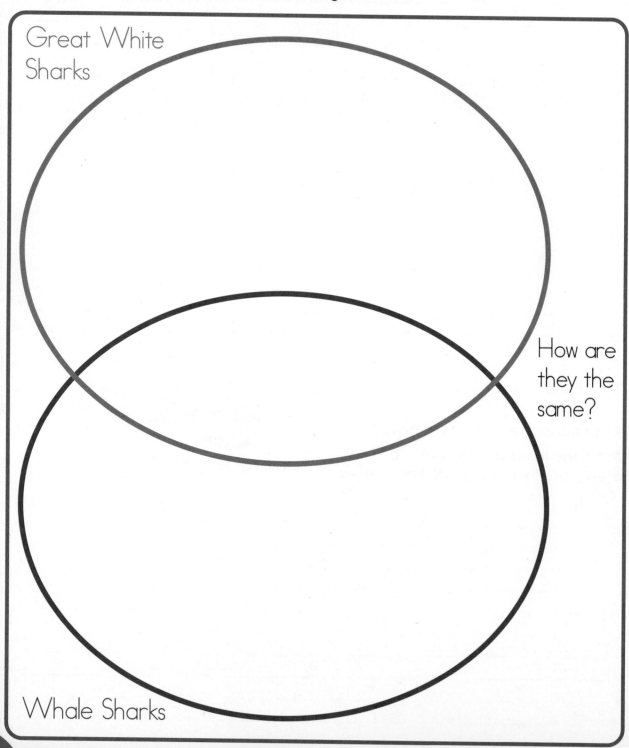

Great White Sharks

How are they the same?

Whale Sharks

# STEM Activity

## The Egg Drop Challenge

Build a parachute and container that will keep an egg safe. It must have a parachute and a container to hold an egg under the parachute. It must be able to protect an egg from breaking in a fall. It must be dropped from at least 10 feet.

## Plan

Explain how you plan to use the materials you are using to make your egg drop parachute on the lines below.

## Design

Draw what you imagine your egg drop parachute will look like in the box. After that, build your egg drop parachute.

# CERTIFICATE
## of Achievement

.....................................

has successfully completed

**LEVEL 6**

Date: .........................

Signed: .........................

# Contractions

A contraction is when two words are combined with an apostrophe. Read the two words in each box and write their contraction on the lines below. Then color the animals.

did not
didn't

was not

have not

is not

I am

he is

she is

it is

I will

you will

they will

she will

123 math

# Regular and Irregular Shapes

A regular shape has all equal sides and all equal angles. An irregular shape has at least one side that is a different length than its other sides and/or at least one different angle than its other angles.

Example:

regular pentagon

irregular pentagon

Circle the correct type for each shape.

## TRIANGLE

regular irregular

regular irregular

## HEXAGON

regular irregular

regular irregular

## OCTAGON

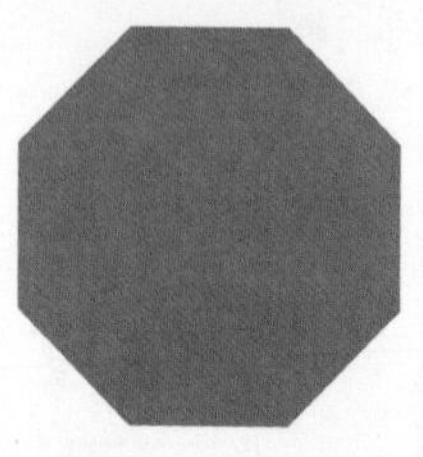

regular irregular

regular irregular

123 math

# Regular and Irregular Shapes

Circle the correct type for each shape.

## QUADRILATERAL

regular irregular

regular irregular

## PENTAGON

regular irregular

regular irregular

## HEPTAGON

regular irregular

regular irregular

## DECAGON

regular irregular

regular irregular

writing

# Writing Sentences

Every sentence starts with a capital letter and ends with a punctuation mark.

Statement sentences tell the reader something. They start with a capital letter and end with a period.

Read the statement sentences. Rewrite them on the lines below using a capital letter at the beginning and ending with a period.

i like to play at the park
let's go swimming today
i live in the United States
the frog jumped over the log
i can feed the chickens on the farm
my name is Emma
i can skate really well

# Shapes and Shares

One half means a figure is partitioned into 2 equal shares.

Example: one whole

1 out of 2 equal shares, or one half

Shade 1 out of 2 equal shares for each shape. Write the missing information below each shape.

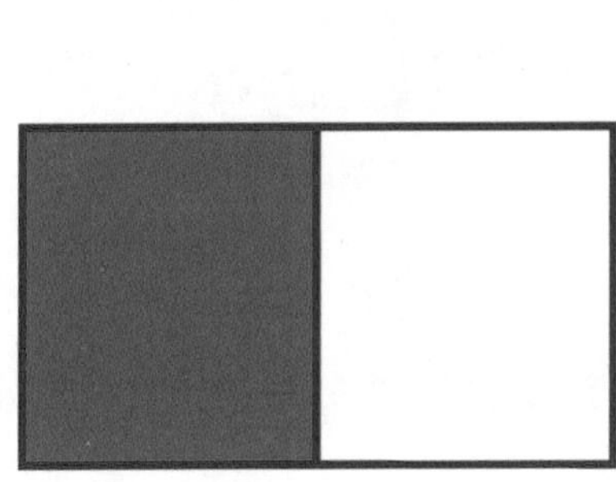

one half of a rectangle

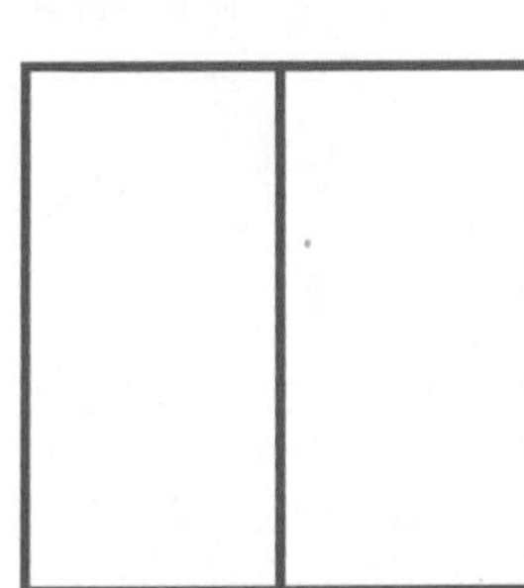

one ______ of a ______________

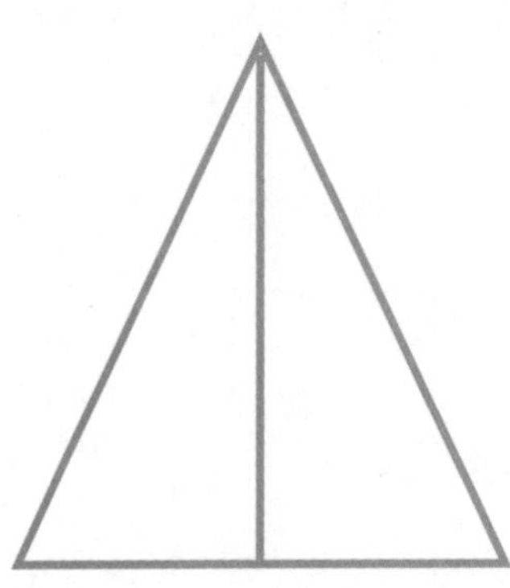

one ______ of a ______________

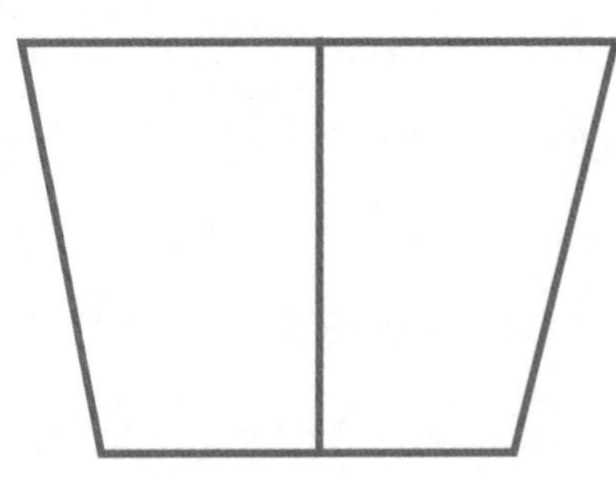

one ______ of a ______________

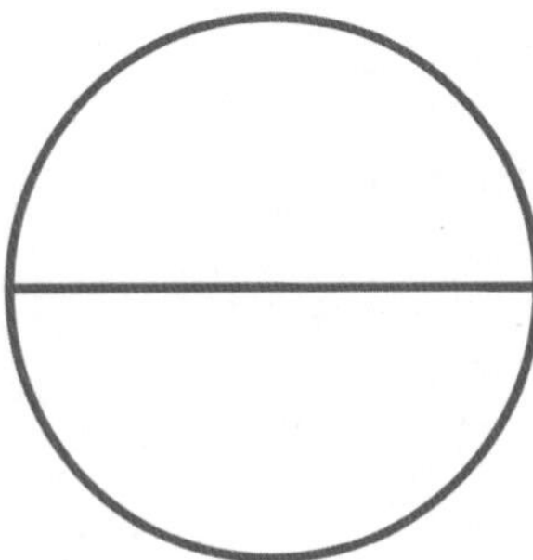

one ______ of a ______________

one ______ of a ______________

# Fiction

Read the story below.

## Monica Goes Camping

Monica was worried. She had been kayaking with her mom and her mom's friends before, but this time it wasn't just for a few hours. They were going kayaking and camping for a whole week!

Monica was worried about being so far from home, sleeping in a tent, and what wild animals might be outside her tent at night! Even though she was worried, she was also excited and felt happy to be invited to go along.

Kayaking was fun on the first day. Monica shared a two-seat kayak with her mom. They paddled for a long time and finally got to the place they were going to camp. It was beautiful. There were no buildings in sight, just big rocks, forest, and clear water.

They all pitched in to set up tents and the campsite. After dinner, they all sat around the campfire and talked and told stories. Then two of the women played guitars, and they all sang songs. Monica and her mom shared a tent and slept soundly after such an active day. They all woke up early and did yoga as the sun came up. They had a good breakfast, packed up camp, and soon were out kayaking again.

As they drove home from the trip, Monica told her mom she couldn't remember what she had been worried about!

# Reading Comprehension

Draw a picture of your favorite part of "Monica Goes Camping."

# Shapes and Shares

One third means a figure is partitioned into 3 equal shares.

Example: one whole | out of 3 equal shares, or one third

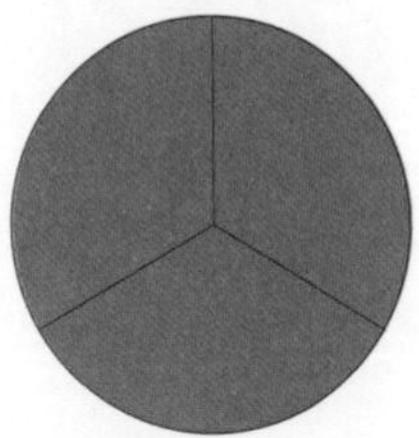

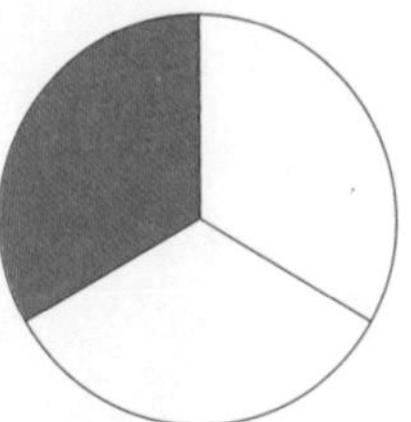

Shade 1 out of 3 equal shares for each shape. Write the missing information below each shape.

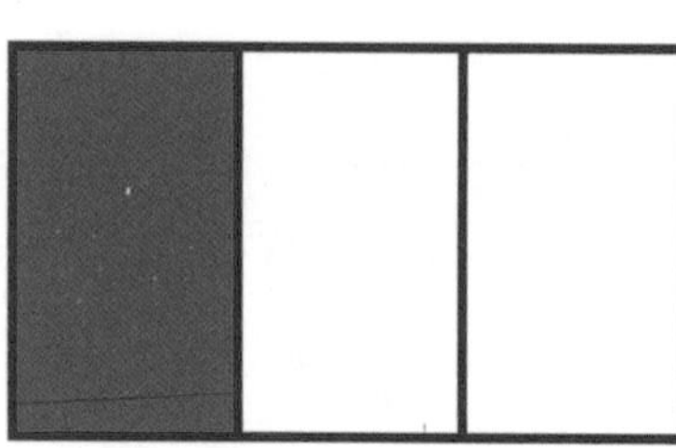

one third of a rectangle

one ______ of a ______________

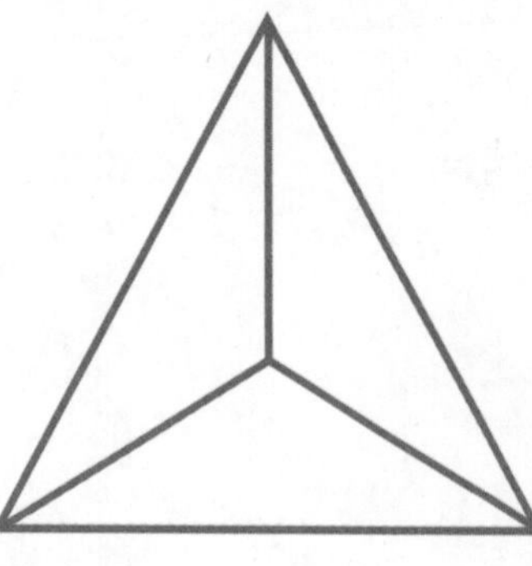

one ______ of a ______________

one ______ of a ______________

# Nonfiction

**Nonfiction text often has photographs and realistic illustrations. They are meant to give the reader a realistic idea of what things actually look like.**

**Sometimes the pictures or illustrations have captions that provide more information about the picture or illustration.**

Butterflies need to live near a water source, such as a stream or pond.

**Use the illustration and caption to answer the questions below.**

What do you see in the illustration?

What does the caption tell you about the illustration?

writing

# Writing Sentences

Question sentences ask the reader a question. They start with a capital letter and end with a question mark.

Read the question sentences. Rewrite them on the lines below using a capital letter at the beginning and ending with a question mark.

what is your favorite sport

do you know how to tie your shoes

can you come out to play today

what is your favorite color

what grade are you in

who is your best friend

where do you live

# Shapes and Shares

One fourth means a figure is partitioned into 4 equal shares.

Example: one whole | 1 out of 4 equal shares, or one fourth

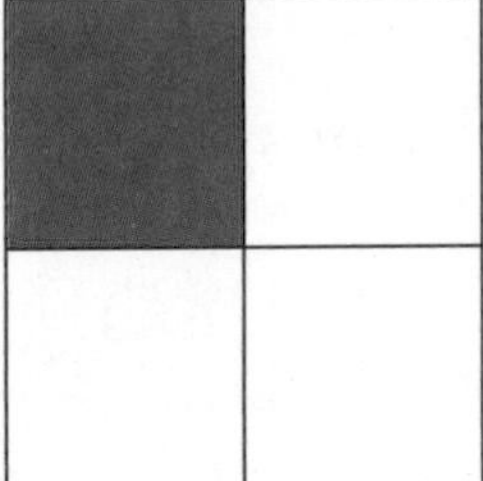

Shade 1 out of 4 equal shares for each shape. Write the missing information below each shape.

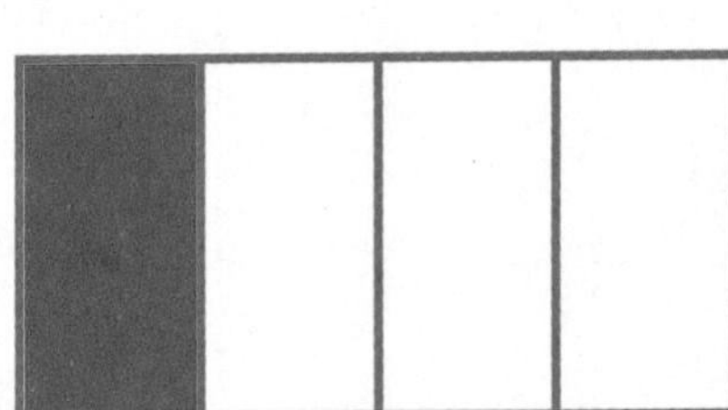

one fourth of a

rectangle

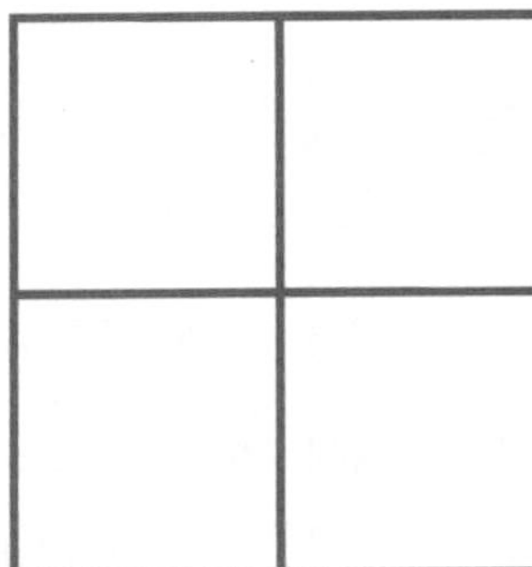

one ________ of a

______________

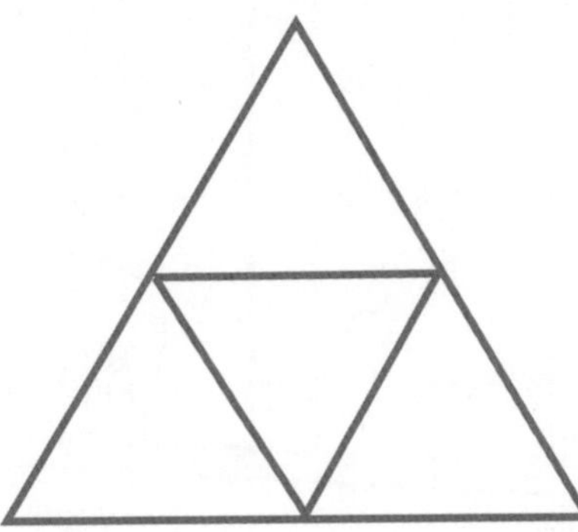

one ________ of a

______________

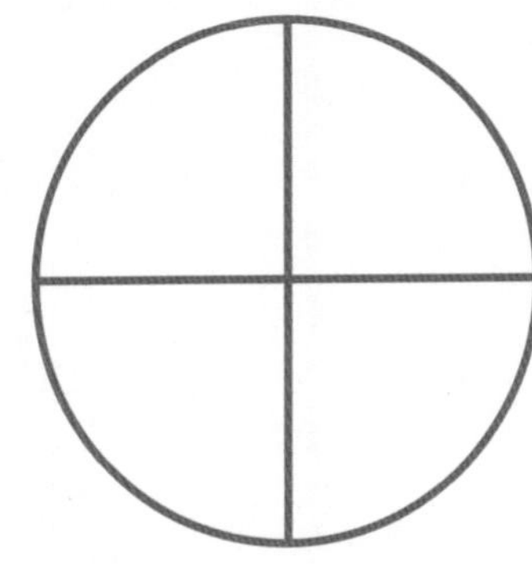

one ________ of a

______________

# Sight Words

There are some words that are hard to sound out because they do not always follow letter-sound rules and do not have picture clues that can help you. Here are some sight words for you to practice reading and writing. Try making up sentences using these words.

**Example:** Where **is the movie playing?**

| | | | |
|---|---|---|---|
| always | don't | or | us |
| around | fast | pull | use |
| another | first | read | very |
| because | five | right | wash |
| been | found | sing | where |
| before | gave | sit | which |
| best | goes | sleep | why |
| both | green | tell | wish |
| buy | it's | their | work |
| call | made | these | would |
| cold | many | those | write |
| does | off | upon | your |

# Sight Word Practice

Look at the beach scene and write about it on the lines below. Use as many sight words as you can from the previous page as you describe what is happening in the scene.

science

# STEM Activity

Engineers and architects create plans for new bridges. Bridges need to be strong to support the weight of cars and people. Try your hand at building a bridge with items you have from home.

## The Challenge

Build a bridge using materials of your choice. It must be at least 4 inches wide and have beams to support it at each end. It can have a center support if you choose. It also must be able to hold an empty cup on top.

## Plan

On the lines below, explain how you plan to use the materials you are using to make your bridge.

## The Design

Draw what you imagine your bridge will look like in the box. After that, build your bridge.

# CERTIFICATE
## of Achievement

........................................

has successfully completed

**LEVEL 7**

Date: ............................

Signed: ............................

reading

# Sight Word Practice

Look at the scene. Create an event and write about it on the lines below. Use sight words you have learned to describe what is happening in the scene. Use the sight words list from page 104.

# Shapes and Area

Area is the amount of surface space inside a flat figure.

Example: All three figures have the same area.

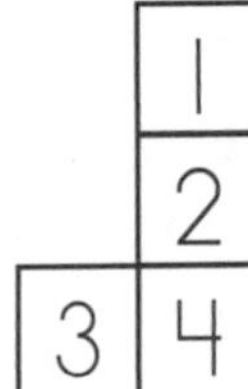


1
2
3 4

4 square units

Write how many square units each object has in its area.

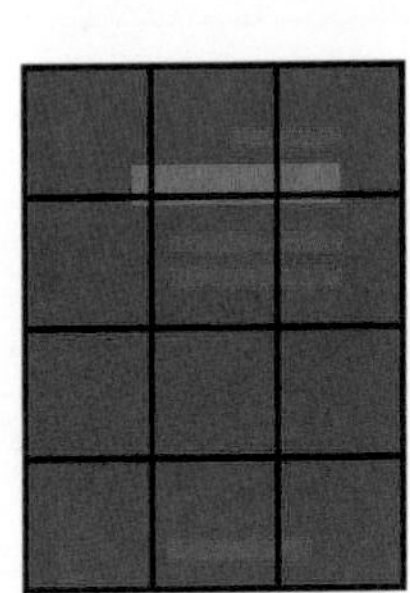

____ square units ____ square units ____ square units

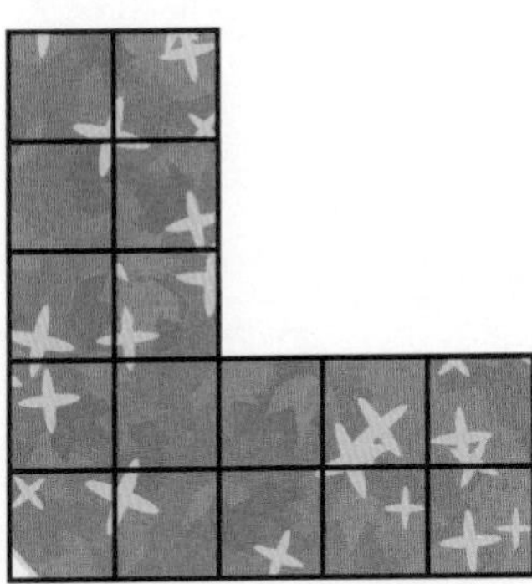

____ square units ____ square unit ____ square units

writing

# Writing Sentences

Exclamation sentences tell the reader about something that is exciting, scary, or surprising. They start with a capital letter and end with an exclamation mark.

Commands are short sentences with only a noun and verb. Commands also start with a capital letter and end with an exclamation mark.

Read the sentences. Rewrite them on the lines below using a capital letter at the beginning and ending with an exclamation mark.

look at that scary monster

i won the race

look at the beautiful fireworks

sit down

go, team

it is my birthday today

look out

# Measurement

Inches are used to measure small things.

Example: The feather is 8 inches long.

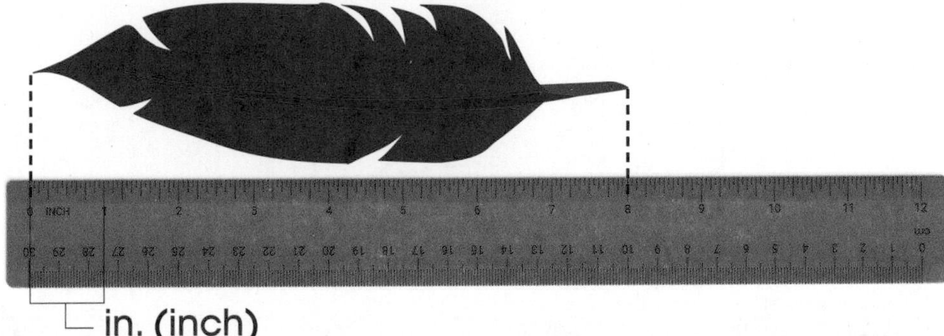


Use the rulers to measure each item in inches. Write the measurements on the lines below.

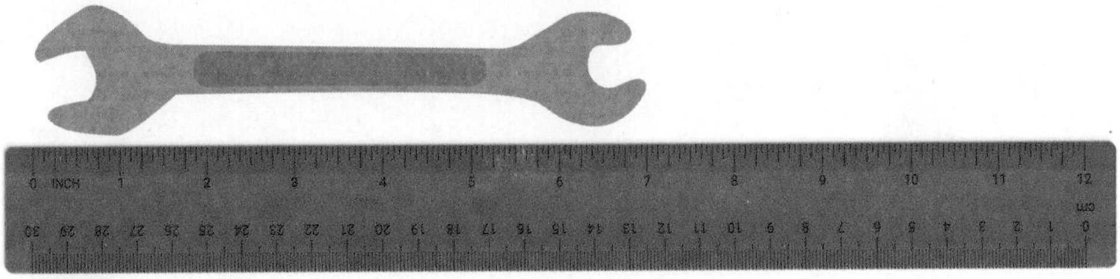

7 in.

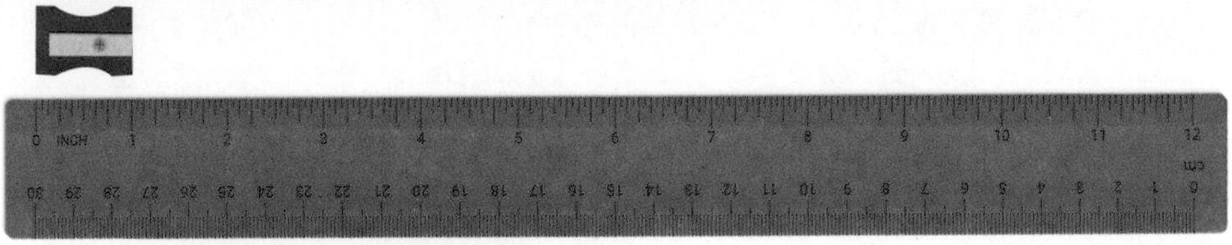

____ in.

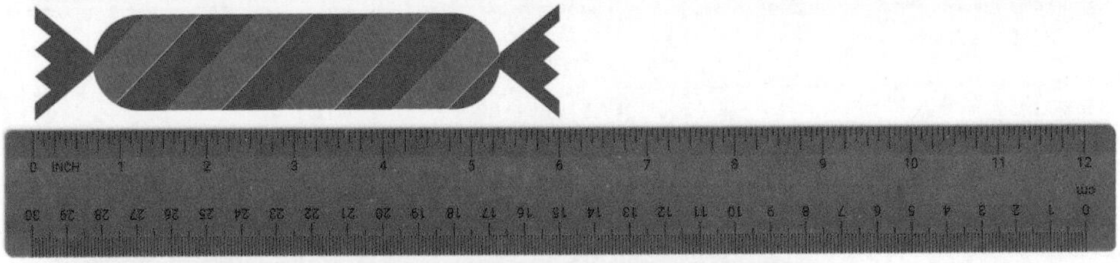

____ in.

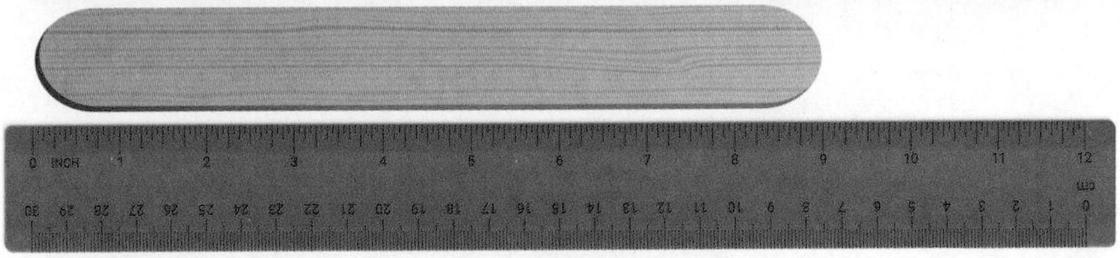

____ in.

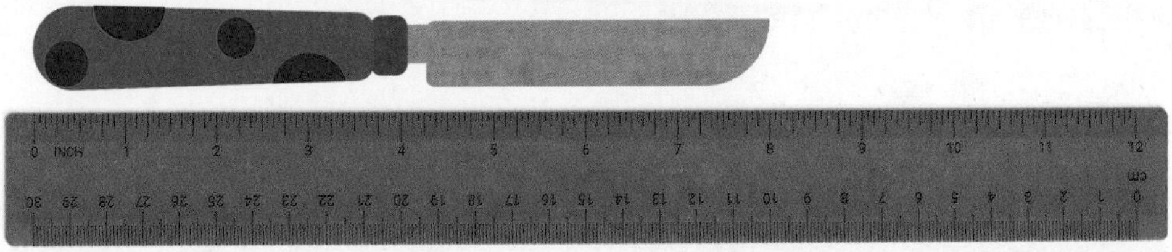

____ in.

# Phonics

The letters er make the r sound. It often comes at the end of a word, but can also be in the middle of a word.

Examples: hammer perch

Read the sentences below. Choose the correct er word from the box above to complete each sentence and write it on the line below.

My brother is ____________ than me.

I wish I could see a ____________ in the ocean.

I have a bandage on my ____________.

I have a little ____________.

My ____________ reads stories to me.

Our mail carrier is a very nice ____________.

My dad climbed a ____________ to paint the house.

Every night my family eats ____________.

# Phonics

The letters ir also make the r sound.

Examples: chirp twirl

Draw a line from the picture to the matching ir word.

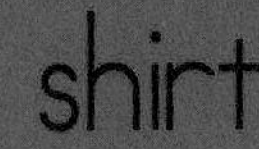

shirt

circus

first

girl

dirt

bird

# Phonics

The letters ur also make the r sound.

Examples: purse hurt

Read the words below. Draw a picture for each ur word.

nurse

burp

surprise

furry

curve

surf

curtain

# Narrative Writing

Narrative writing is writing a story with a beginning, middle, and end.

**Complete the graphic organizer below to help you brainstorm ideas. Think of a time you played with a friend. What happened first? What happened next? What happened then? And what happened last? Draw pictures or write a few idea words in each box to plan your story writing.**

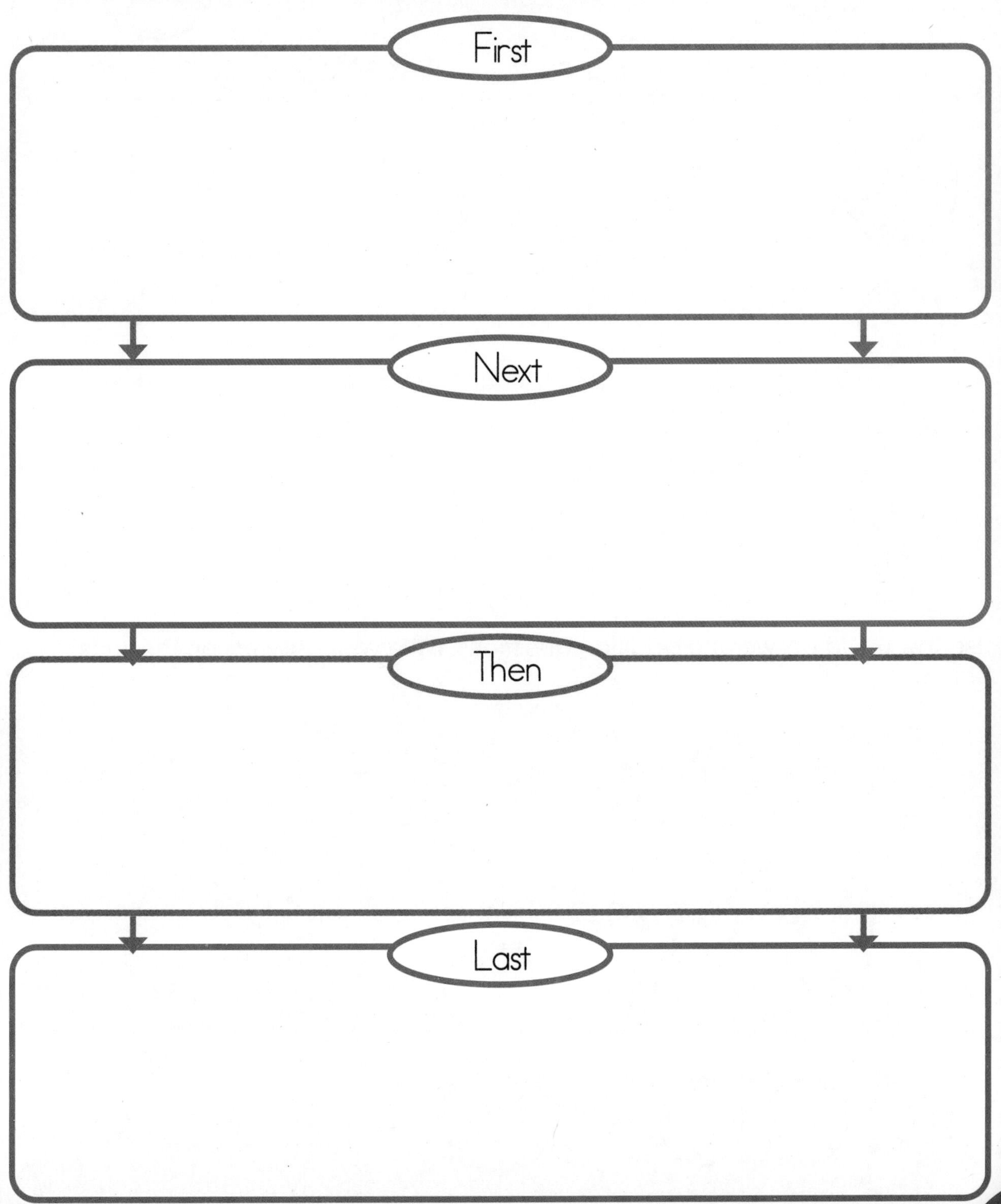

math

# Money

Use the key below and draw a line from each coin to the piggy bank with the correct total.

Key:

|  |  |  |  |
|---|---|---|---|
| 1 cent | 5 cents | 10 cents | 25 cents |

Use the key to answer the addition questions. Write your answers on the lines below.

 + = ________¢

  + = ________¢

   +  

# Time

Every 15 minutes is one quarter of an hour.

When the minute hand is on the 3, it is 15 minutes past, or a quarter past, the hour.

When the minute hand is on the 6, it is 30 minutes past, or half past, the hour.

When the minute hand is on the 9, it is 45 minutes past, or a quarter to, the next hour.

45 minutes after the hour (quarter to)

15 minutes after the hour (quarter past)

30 minutes after the hour (half past)

Write the time under the clocks below.

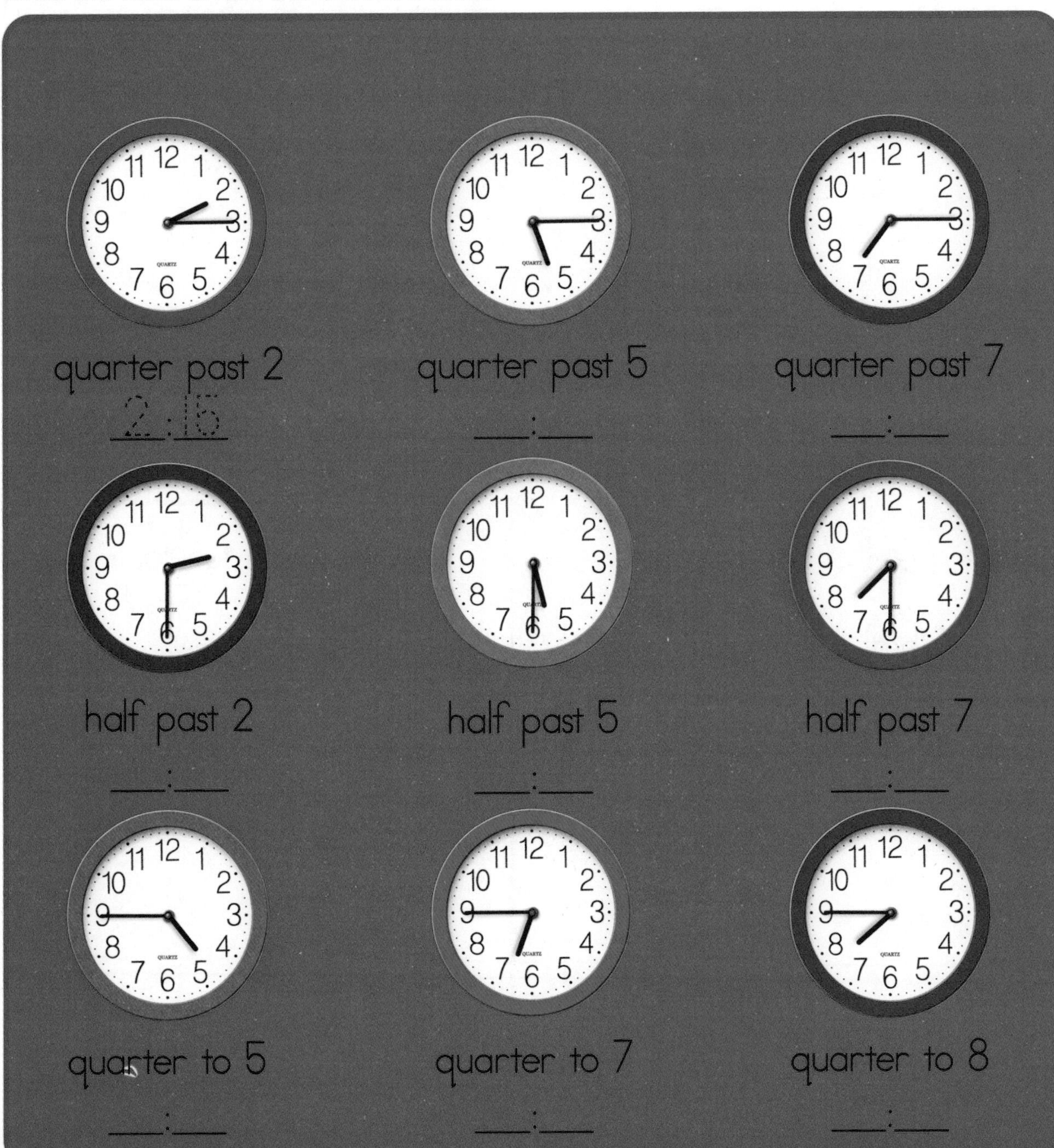

# Informational Writing

Informational writing **is writing about** a topic **and** providing details **to help readers** understand more about the topic.

**Write about an animal that you know a lot about. Draw pictures or write a few words about it in the graphic organizer below to organize your thoughts.**

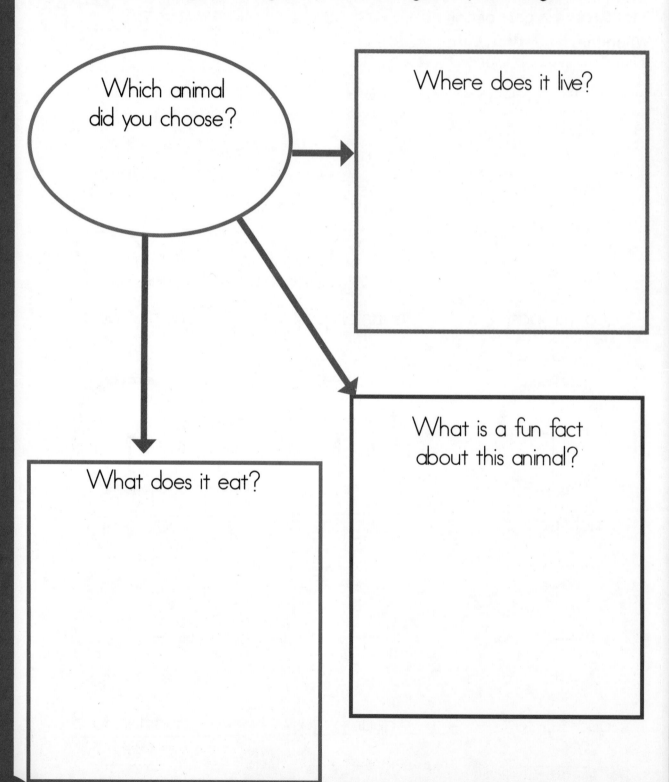

Which animal did you choose?

Where does it live?

What does it eat?

What is a fun fact about this animal?

123 math

# Time

What time is it? Write the time under each clock. Note that each number on a clock represents 5 minutes.

What time is it? Draw the hands on the clocks to match the digital times.

# Time

Draw a line from the digital clock to its matching analog clock.

Example: digital analog

# Data Management

A picture graph **uses** pictures to represent units. **The** key **tells you the** unit quantity.

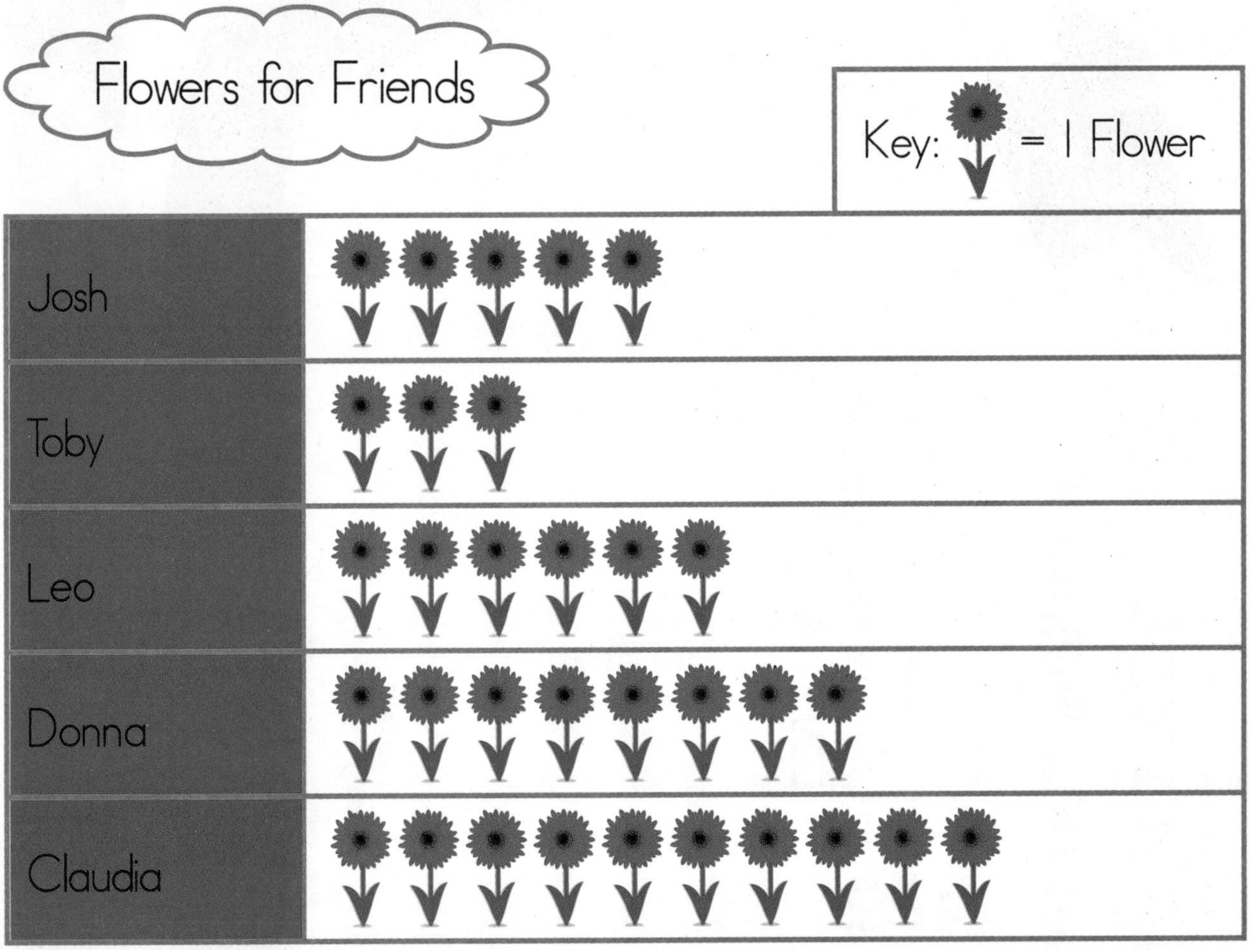

## Flowers for Friends

Key: (flower) = 1 Flower

| | |
| --- | --- |
| Josh | 🌻🌻🌻🌻🌻 |
| Toby | 🌻🌻🌻 |
| Leo | 🌻🌻🌻🌻🌻🌻 |
| Donna | 🌻🌻🌻🌻🌻🌻🌻🌻 |
| Claudia | 🌻🌻🌻🌻🌻🌻🌻🌻🌻🌻 |

**Use the picture graph to answer the questions about the data. Write your answers on the lines below.**

How many more flowers does Josh have than Toby? ________

How many flowers do Leo and Claudia have combined? _____

How many fewer flowers does Leo have than Donna? ______

How many flowers do the friends have if they put all their flowers in one vase? ________

# CERTIFICATE
## of Achievement

..........................................

has successfully completed

**LEVEL 8**

Date: ............................

Signed: ............................

writing

# ABC Order

Putting words into ABC order means they are in the order of the alphabet. If there are multiple words with the same first letter, you need to look at the second letter and sometimes the third letter to put the words in the correct alphabetical order.

Example: diamond dog doughnut

Diamond is the first word in ABC order because i comes before o in the alphabet. The remaining two words both have an o after the first letter. Dog is the next word in ABC order because g comes before u in the alphabet. The last word in ABC order is doughnut.

Put all the words in ABC order. Then rewrite them all in order on the lines below.

# Vocabulary

A syllable is a word or part of a word that is heard when you make one clap.

Example:

1 syllable
bear
2 syllables
li/on
3 syllables
el/e/phant


Read the words below out loud as you clap each syllable. How many syllables do you hear? Sort the words into the correct categories based on the number of claps you hear. Write them on the lines below.

wolf pelican monkey snake kangaroo whale
porcupine turtle giraffe octopus walrus seal

| 1 SYLLABLE | 2 SYLLABLES | 3 SYLLABLES |
|---|---|---|
| | | |
| | | |
| | | |
| | | |

# Number Sense

Put the numbers in order from least to greatest. Use place value or the value of each digit in the number to determine the order. Write the numbers on the lines below.

Example:

| | |
|---|---|
| 2,432 1,567 3,253 7,119 | _____, _____, _____, _____ |
| 6,547 1,734 5,087 2,891 | _____, _____, _____, _____ |
| 2,322 1,845 4,137 7,678 | _____, _____, _____, _____ |
| 4,688 4,156 3,273 5,449 | _____, _____, _____, _____ |
| 9,555 5,381 1,291 8,762 | _____, _____, _____, _____ |

Find the numbers that match the descriptions. Write the numbers on the lines below.

| | | |
|---|---|---|
| 2,625 | 4,275 | 1,439 |
| 7,443 | 6,217 | 5,000 |

The number between 2,000 and 3,000 is 2,625.

The number that has 0 tens and 0 ones is __________.

The number between 1,000 and 1,500 is __________.

The number between 4,000 and 5,000 is __________.

The number that has 7 ones is __________.

The number greater than all the others numbers is __________.

# Grammar

Homophones are words that have the same pronunciation but different spellings and different meanings.

Example:  sun and son 

Look at the pictures below and circle the correct homophone word.

see sea

ate eight

bear bare

flour flower

be bee

deer dear

Each sentence below has a word in it that is the wrong homophone. Circle the incorrect homophone and write the correct one on the line after the sentence.

I bought a new (pear) of shoes today! pair

Eye am going skating at the rink tonight. ____________

Let's right a letter to a friend. ____________

I can't weight for my birthday party next week. ____________

Did you sea that shooting star in the sky? ____________

I'm going to pick some flours for my mom. ____________

# Vocabulary

If you are not certain how to read a word, it may help you to figure out the word's syllables, or chunks. A helpful hint is to remember that there will usually be at least one vowel (A, E, I, O, U, and sometimes Y) in each syllable in a word.

Example: dif/ /fer/ /ent

Break these words into syllables based on the vowels in each chunk and write how many syllables each word has on the line across from each word. Use a colored pencil to show the division of the words.

| | |
|---|---|
| h o l/i/d a y | 3 syllables |
| s n o w m a n | ______ syllables |
| h a l l w a y | ______ syllables |
| g a r d e n | ______ syllables |
| t o g e t h e r | ______ syllables |
| w i n t e r | ______ syllables |
| s k a t i n g | ______ syllables |
| e x p e r i m e n t | ______ syllables |
| e x c i t e d | ______ syllables |
| s c i e n t i s t | ______ syllables |

# Number Sense

**Use the models below to count and write how many thousands, hundreds, tens, and ones there are on the lines below.**

Example:

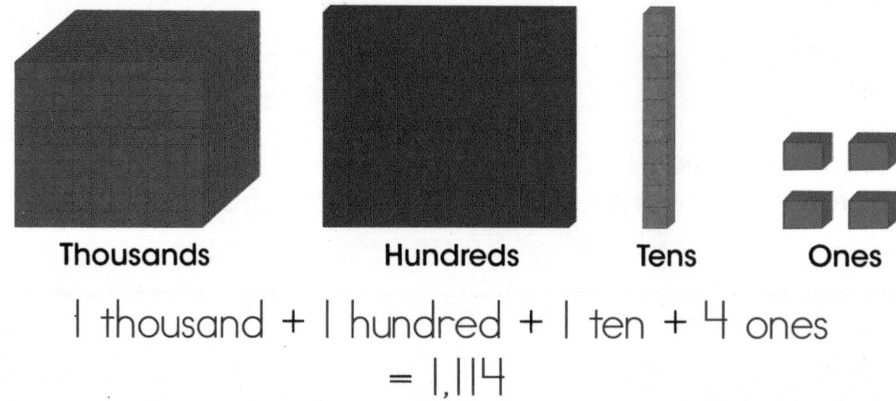


1 thousand + 1 hundred + 1 ten + 4 ones
= 1,114

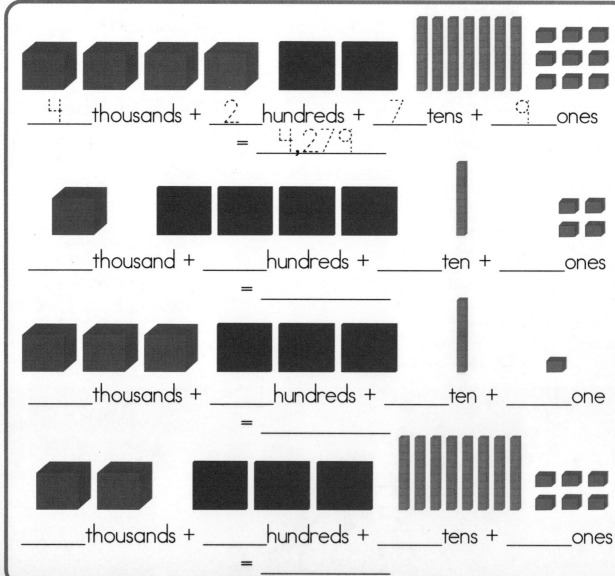

__4__ thousands + __2__ hundreds + __7__ tens + __9__ ones
= __4,279__

______ thousand + ______ hundreds + ______ ten + ______ ones
= __________

______ thousands + ______ hundreds + ______ ten + ______ one
= __________

______ thousands + ______ hundreds + ______ tens + ______ ones
= __________

# Grammar

Homographs are words that have the same spelling, but different pronunciations and different meanings.

Example:  bass and bass 

Look at the two pictures in each box below. Write the correct homograph to complete the two sentences in each box.

I like the pretty ______ in your hair.

A ______ can be a sign of respect.

The ________ is blowing very hard!

My brother will ________ up the toy.

A ___________ landed on my windowsill!

Jason ___________ into the cold water.

# Vocabulary

**If you don't know the meaning of a word in a sentence, knowing the meanings of the other words in the sentence can help you understand the unknown word.**

**Example:** I packed the apples in my bag, but I excluded some because they had bruises on them.

**Excluded means separated or taken away, so some of the apples didn't go into the bag because they had bruises on them.**

**Read each sentence below. What does each word in red mean? Underline the words in the sentence that help you figure out the meaning of that word. Write your own definition of the word on the lines below each sentence.**

I ate too much candy, and now my stomach feels queasy.

I saw a gigantic giraffe at the zoo. It was as tall as a tree!

We built a tower so high that it wobbled, and then it toppled over.

I was sneezing, so my dad gave me a handkerchief for my nose.

Nothing scares my little brother because he is so adventurous.

We are so eager to go to the birthday party on Friday night!

# Number Sense

Sometimes we use rounding to make an estimate to tell about how much a number is. When you round, you take the number to the nearest ten, hundred, or thousand, etc. Take a look at the number line to see how you can use it to help you understand rounding.

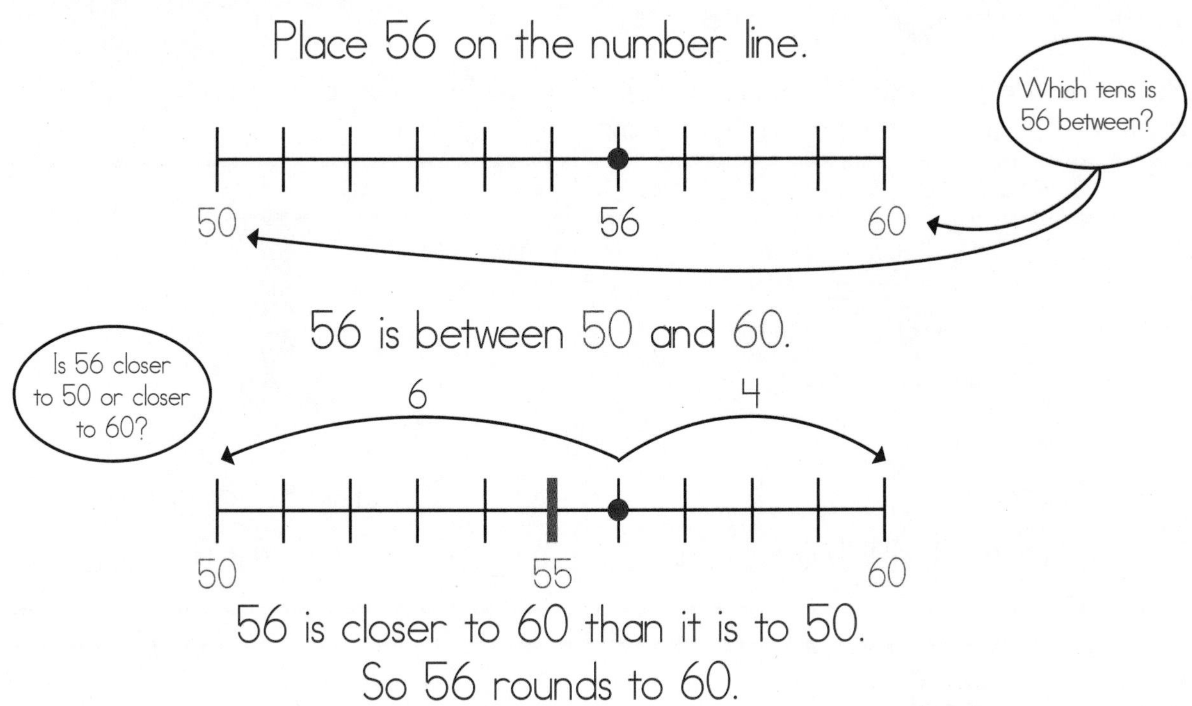

Place 56 on the number line.
Which tens is 56 between?
50
56
60
56 is between 50 and 60.
Is 56 closer to 50 or closer to 60?
6
4
50
55
60
56 is closer to 60 than it is to 50.
So 56 rounds to 60.


HINT: If the number in the ones place is equal to or greater than 5, round up to the next ten. If the number is less than 5, round down.

Use the number line to help you round. Read the numbers and mark them on the number lines with a dot. Then round to the nearest ten and write your answers on the lines below.

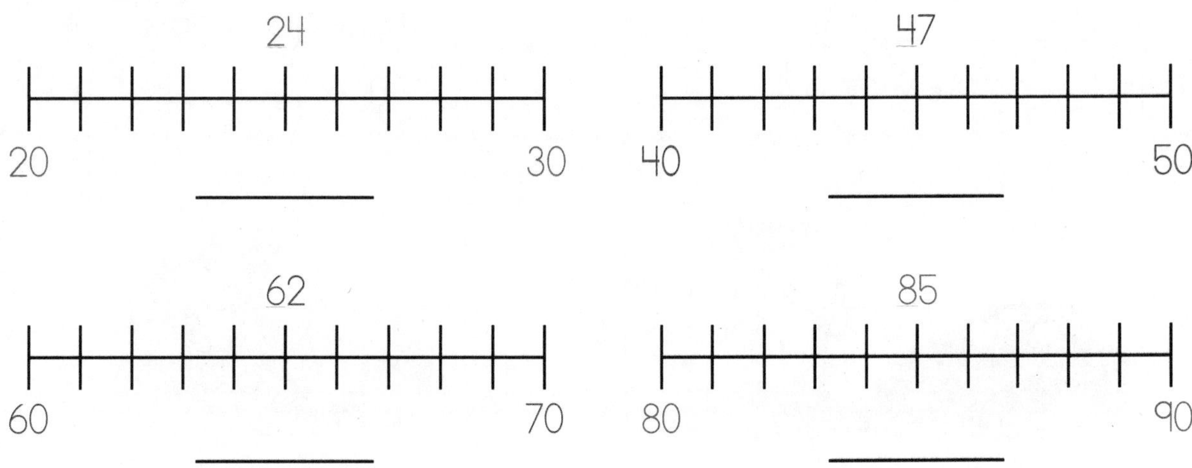


Round to the nearest ten. Write the answers on the lines.

57 ________ 34 ________ 82 ________ 75 ________

# Grammar

Homonyms are words that have the same pronunciation and the same spelling but have different meanings.

Example: 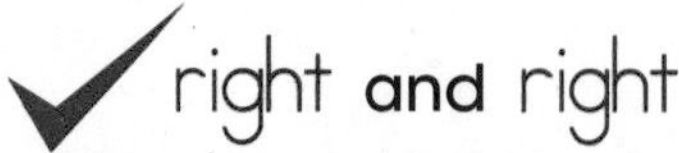 right and right 

Look at the two pictures in each box below. Write the correct homonym to complete the two sentences in each box.

I wrote a ________ to my best friend.

"I" is a word and a ________ of the alphabet.

A ________ tree can grow very tall.

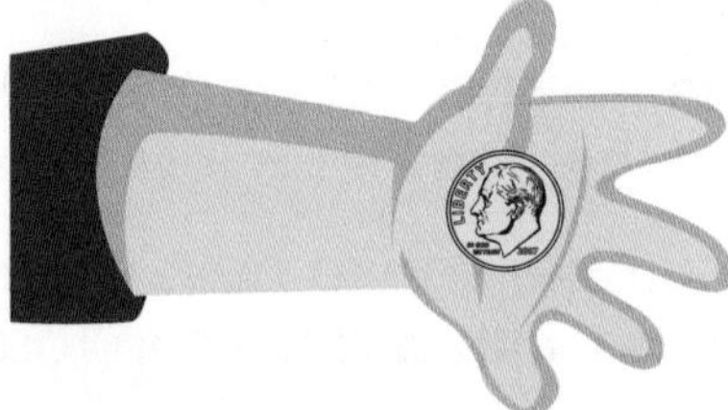

I have ten cents in my ________.

My dad will ________ our car.

I love to play at the ________.

# Reading Comprehension

Follow the directions below to complete the neighborhood map.

1. Draw an American flag on a pole in front of the post office.
2. Draw your house in the southeast corner of the map.
3. Draw two children beside the school.
4. Draw a fire truck inside of the fire station.
5. Draw a car on Main Street driving toward the gas station.
6. Draw a librarian at the library holding a book.
7. Draw yourself on Orange Street near your house.

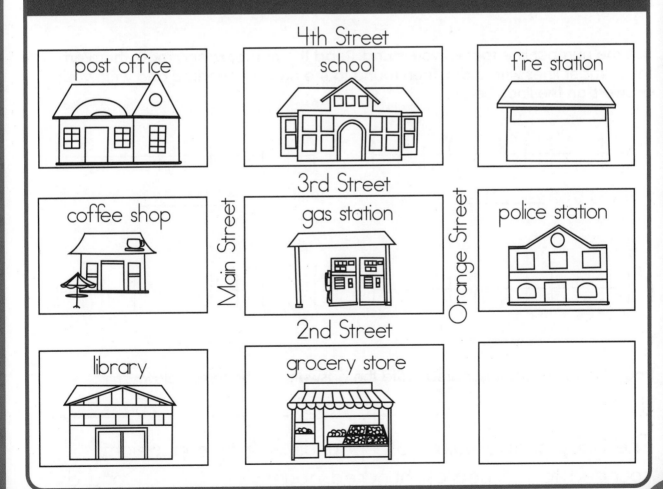

4th Street

| post office | school | fire station |
|---|---|---|

3rd Street

| coffee shop | Main Street / gas station | Orange Street / police station |
|---|---|---|

2nd Street

| library | grocery store | |
|---|---|---|

# Number Sense

You can use what you learned from rounding to the nearest ten to help you round to the nearest hundred. Use the number line to help you know when to round up or round down. Remember, rounding is used to make an estimate.

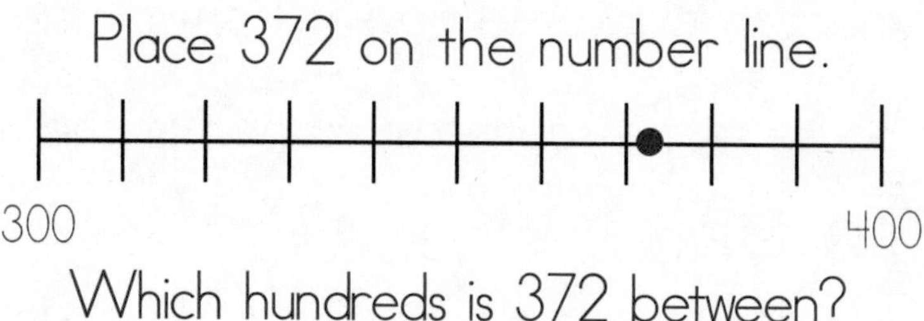

Place 372 on the number line.
300
400
Which hundreds is 372 between?

To round, ask yourself if 372 is closer to 300 or 400. It is closer to 400, so 372 rounds to 400. You can also look at the number in the tens place. If the number is equal to or greater than 50, you will round up. 372 has 70 in the tens place, which is greater than 50, so it needs to be rounded up to 400.

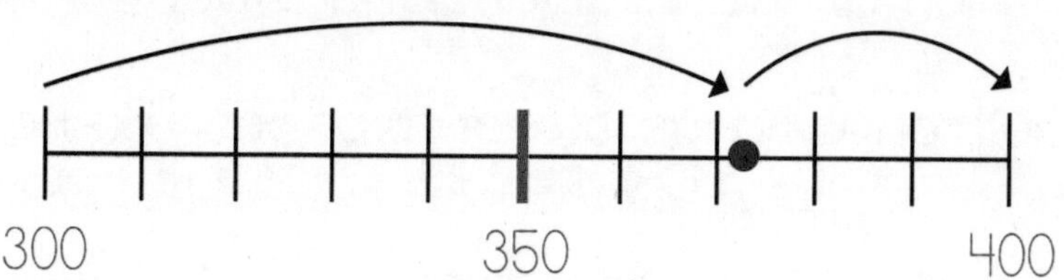


Use the number line to help you round. Read the numbers and mark them on the number lines with a dot. Then round to the nearest hundred and write your answers on the lines below.

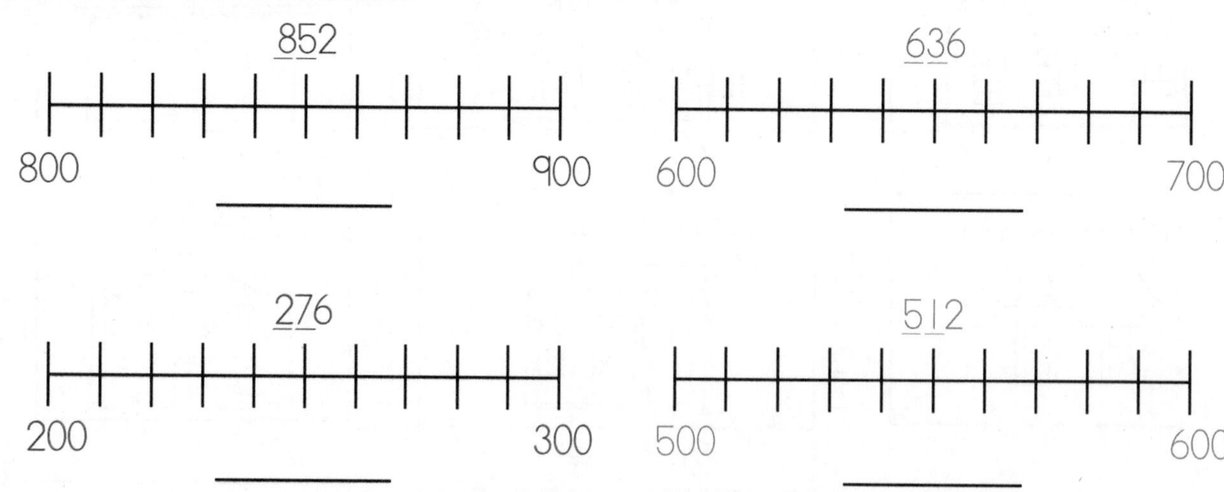


Round to the nearest hundred. Write the answers on the lines below.

467 ________ 298 ________ 553 ________ 725 ________

The baby giraffe weighs 341 pounds. What is its weight rounded to the nearest hundred pounds? ________ pounds

# Grammar

Comparative adverbs are used when comparing two of something.

A comparative adverb may be a:

- single word
- one-syllable adverb with -er suffix
- phrase

**Example:** A sundae tastes better than an ice pop. A cheetah is faster than a lion. Dominic paints less carefully than Randall.

| worse | more cheaply | longer | as slowly as |
|---|---|---|---|
| less | more seriously | later | as quickly as |

**Read each sentence below. Use the comparative adverbs in the table above to complete the sentences.**

1. The box is ________________ than it is tall.

2. Did William finish the race ______________________ his brother?

3. Getting sick is ________________ than getting a shot.

4. The movie starts ________________ than the game.

5. Candice took the dance contest _____________________ than Joseph.

6. The soup did not boil ______________________ the stew.

7. The shirt fabric was made _________________________ than the coat fabric.

8. The remote control car costs _________________ than the bicycle.

# STEM Activity

Use your engineering skills to build a small rocking chair!

## The Challenge

Build a rocking chair using materials of your choice. It must be at least 10 inches tall and has to be able to rock while holding a small toy figure of your choice.

## Plan

On the lines below, explain how you plan to use the materials you are using to make your rocking chair.

## The Design

Draw what you imagine the rocking chair will look like in the box. After that, build your rocking chair.

# CERTIFICATE

## of Achievement

..............................................

has successfully completed

**LEVEL 9**

Date:

Signed:

..............................  ..............................

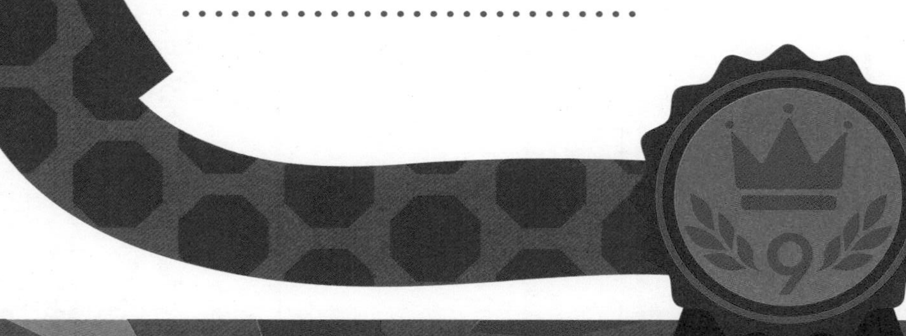

123 math

# Addition and Subtraction

You can use place value to help you add multi-digit numbers when you need to regroup.

Example: 256 + 538 = 200 + 50 + 6

500 + 30 + 8

700 + 80 + 14 = 794

Solve the equations below by using the place-value strategy and write the answers on the lines.

126 + 147 =

____ + ____ + ____

____ + ____ + ____

____ + ____ + ____ = ____

245 + 537 =

____ + ____ + ____

____ + ____ + ____

____ + ____ + ____ = ____

708 + 213 =

____ + ____ + ____

____ + ____ + ____

____ + ____ + ____ = ____

279 + 610 =

____ + ____ + ____

____ + ____ + ____

____ + ____ + ____ = ____

324 + 437 =

____ + ____ + ____

____ + ____ + ____

____ + ____ + ____ = ____

436 + 355 =

____ + ____ + ____

____ + ____ + ____

____ + ____ + ____ = ____

Solve the word problem by using the place-value strategy and write the equation and the sum on the lines.

Alison is having a big party! She has 178 red party hats and 312 blue party hats. How many hats does Alison have for her party?

____ + ____ + ____

____ + ____ + ____

____ + ____ + ____ = ____

123 math

# Addition and Subtraction

**Adding hundreds, tens, and ones sometimes involves regrouping. If the numbers in a column add up to more than 9, you need to regroup to the next higher place value.**

**Practice adding and subtracting three-digit numbers. Write the answers in the boxes below.**

| | Hundreds | Tens | Ones |
|---|---|---|---|
| | 3 | 2 | 1 |
| + | 4 | 3 | 7 |
| | | | |

| | Hundreds | Tens | Ones |
|---|---|---|---|
| | 4 | 2 | 6 |
| - | 3 | 1 | 3 |
| | | | |

| | Hundreds | Tens | Ones |
|---|---|---|---|
| | 7 | 0 | 3 |
| + | 1 | 1 | 3 |
| | | | |

| | Hundreds | Tens | Ones |
|---|---|---|---|
| | 7 | 1 | 4 |
| - | 5 | 1 | 3 |
| | | | |

| | Hundreds | Tens | Ones |
|---|---|---|---|
| | 2 | 9 | 9 |
| - | 1 | 0 | 7 |
| | | | |

| | Hundreds | Tens | Ones |
|---|---|---|---|
| | 4 | 6 | 2 |
| + | 3 | 1 | 6 |
| | | | |

| | Hundreds | Tens | Ones |
|---|---|---|---|
| | 6 | 3 | 7 |
| - | 5 | 2 | 2 |
| | | | |

| | Hundreds | Tens | Ones |
|---|---|---|---|
| | 4 | 3 | 6 |
| + | 2 | 6 | 2 |
| | | | |

| | Hundreds | Tens | Ones |
|---|---|---|---|
| | 5 | 5 | 3 |
| - | 4 | 3 | 2 |
| | | | |

**Answer the number sense questions and write your answers on the lines.**

What number is in the tens place of the number 274? ______

What number is in the ones place of the number 680? ______

What number is in the hundreds place of the number 175? ______

How many tens are in the number 369? ______

writing

# Word Relationships

**Nuance** means a slightly different meaning about the same topic or idea. Words can be grouped based on a topic or idea from the **least** to the **greatest** intensity based on each word's meaning.

**Example:** When you think about describing someone "trying to get someone else's attention," the word meaning nuances from least to greatest could be:

| Least | Greater | Still Greater | Greatest |
|---|---|---|---|
| whisper | call | holler | scream |

**Order each word set below from least to greatest intensity for each topic below.**

Topic: move from one place to another
Word Set: run, stroll, walk, jog

| Least | Greater | Still Greater | Greatest |
|---|---|---|---|
| | | | |

Topic: reaction to a birthday party
Word Set: exciting, great, nice, amazing

| Least | Greater | Still Greater | Greatest |
|---|---|---|---|
| | | | |

Topic: how someone might feel at the end of a long day at school
Word Set: exhausted, fatigued, tired, worn-out

| Least | Greater | Still Greater | Greatest |
|---|---|---|---|
| | | | |

Topic: motion of an object moving from one person to another
Word Set: hurl, toss, throw, fling

| Least | Greater | Still Greater | Greatest |
|---|---|---|---|
| | | | |

123 math

# Addition and Subtraction

**Adding hundreds, tens, and ones sometimes involves regrouping. If the numbers in a column add up to more than 9, you need to regroup to the next higher place value.**

**Practice adding and subtracting three-digit numbers. Write the answers in the boxes below.**

| | Hundreds | Tens | Ones |
|---|---|---|---|
| | 4 | 3 | 9 |
| - | 3 | 1 | 5 |
| | | | |

| | Hundreds | Tens | Ones |
|---|---|---|---|
| | 1 | 4 | 3 |
| + | 3 | 4 | 5 |
| | | | |

| | Hundreds | Tens | Ones |
|---|---|---|---|
| | 9 | 5 | 6 |
| - | 6 | 2 | 6 |
| | | | |

| | Hundreds | Tens | Ones |
|---|---|---|---|
| | 5 | 1 | 1 |
| + | 3 | 0 | 0 |
| | | | |

| | Hundreds | Tens | Ones |
|---|---|---|---|
| | 7 | 5 | 3 |
| - | 2 | 1 | 3 |
| | | | |

| | Hundreds | Tens | Ones |
|---|---|---|---|
| | 8 | 4 | 9 |
| + | 1 | 3 | 0 |
| | | | |

| | Hundreds | Tens | Ones |
|---|---|---|---|
| | 9 | 8 | 9 |
| - | 5 | 6 | 3 |
| | | | |

| | Hundreds | Tens | Ones |
|---|---|---|---|
| | 1 | 2 | 3 |
| + | 1 | 2 | 3 |
| | | | |

| | Hundreds | Tens | Ones |
|---|---|---|---|
| | 6 | 4 | 5 |
| - | 3 | 4 | 5 |
| | | | |

**Answer the number sense questions and write your answers on the lines.**

What number is in the hundreds place of the number 867? ______

How many tens are in the number 134? ______

What number is in the tens place of the number 657? ______

How many ones are in the number 979? ______

reading

# Reading Comprehension

Sequencing is putting directions in the correct order.

You can sequence the order of any activity.

**Read the steps for building a snowman below. Write the numbers in the boxes to put the steps in order and then rewrite the steps in the correct order on the lines below.**

Give your snowman a hat and scarf. ☐

Roll one small, one medium, and one large snowball. ☐

Put a stick on each side of the medium snowball for arms. ☐

Place the small snowball on top of the medium snowball. ☐

Put a mouth, button eyes, and a carrot nose on the small snowball. ☐

Place the medium snowball on top of the large snowball. ☐

1. ______________________________

2. ______________________________

3. ______________________________

4. ______________________________

5. ______________________________

6. ______________________________

# Addition and Subtraction

**Adding hundreds, tens, and ones sometimes involves regrouping. If the numbers in a column add up to more than 9, you need to regroup to the next higher place value.**

**Solve the problems by regrouping. Write the answers in the boxes below.**

| | Hundreds | Tens | Ones |
|---|---|---|---|
| | | 1 | |
| | 1 | 2 | 6 |
| + | 1 | 4 | 7 |
| | 2 | 7 | 3 |

| | Hundreds | Tens | Ones |
|---|---|---|---|
| | | | |
| | 2 | 4 | 5 |
| + | 5 | 3 | 7 |
| | | | |

| | Hundreds | Tens | Ones |
|---|---|---|---|
| | | | |
| | 3 | 2 | 4 |
| + | 4 | 3 | 7 |
| | | | |

| | Hundreds | Tens | Ones |
|---|---|---|---|
| | | | |
| | 4 | 6 | 5 |
| + | 3 | 1 | 6 |
| | | | |

| | Hundreds | Tens | Ones |
|---|---|---|---|
| | | | |
| | 7 | 0 | 8 |
| + | 2 | 1 | 3 |
| | | | |

| | Hundreds | Tens | Ones |
|---|---|---|---|
| | | | |
| | 4 | 3 | 6 |
| + | 3 | 6 | 5 |
| | | | |

| | Hundreds | Tens | Ones |
|---|---|---|---|
| | | | |
| | 5 | 3 | 6 |
| + | 2 | 1 | 6 |
| | | | |

| | Hundreds | Tens | Ones |
|---|---|---|---|
| | | | |
| | 2 | 7 | 9 |
| + | 6 | 4 | 4 |
| | | | |

| | Hundreds | Tens | Ones |
|---|---|---|---|
| | | | |
| | 2 | 5 | 6 |
| + | 4 | 1 | 6 |
| | | | |

**Solve the word problem and write the equation and the sum in the box.**

Olivia is also having a big party! She is buying party hats for everyone. She buys 178 silver party hats and 352 gold party hats. How many party hats did Olivia buy altogether?

| | Hundreds | Tens | Ones |
|---|---|---|---|
| | | | |
| | | | |
| + | | | |
| | | | |

# Titles

Movie titles, book titles, and titles of plays or poems are written using a capital letter for almost every word in the title. Only the small words, such as the, to, in, if, and, or, and on are not capitalized, unless one of those words comes at the beginning or end of the title.

Example: Humpty Dumpty

Aladdin and the Magic Lamp

Look at the three movie posters below. Write the title next to each movie poster using correct capitalization.

Coming Soon:

Write your own book title on the lines below. Be sure to capitalize it properly.

# Reading Comprehension

The main idea is what the story is mainly about.

Example: A book titled *Tammy's First Bus Ride* is probably about a bus ride. That is the main idea.

Read the passage.

Anthony and Rebecca love to travel. They have flown to many different countries around the world and have loved every one of them. Their favorite country to visit was Spain, but they also loved France and Japan.

Circle the main idea.

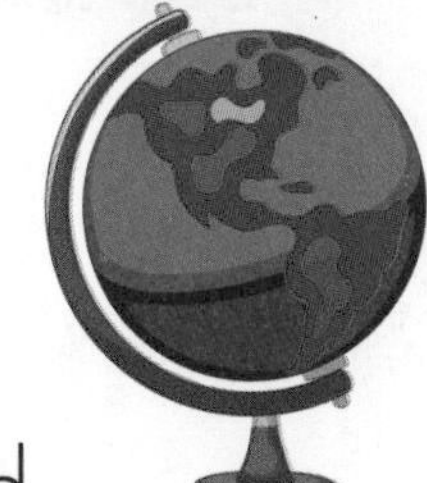

- Anthony and Rebecca's favorite country is Spain.
- Anthony and Rebecca have traveled to France.
- Anthony and Rebecca enjoy traveling around the world.

Barry and Marion rode their bikes to the grocery store. They bought all of their favorite candy and snacks. Barry likes chocolate, and Marion likes pretzels. They decided to share their treats. Marion discovered that she likes chocolate, and Barry found out that he likes pretzels!

Circle the main idea.

- Marion likes pretzels.
- Barry and Marion rode their bikes to the grocery store.
- Barry and Marion tried new snacks and liked them.

# Grammar

**Superlative adjectives are used when comparing three or more nouns. Superlative adjectives are also used when comparing one thing to a group.**

**Example:** Jupiter is the biggest planet in the solar system.
That was the best movie ever made!

| fastest | most happy | least important | worst |
|---|---|---|---|
| deepest | most famous | least sweet | best |

**Read each sentence below. Use the superlative adjectives in the table above to complete the sentences.**

1. The furry dog was the ________________ when we came into the room.
2. What is the ____________ ocean in the world?
3. I think chocolate is the __________ flavor of ice cream!
4. I think the __________ chore is having to take out smelly garbage!
5. What pitcher has thrown the ______________ pitch ever?
6. This pie is the __________________ of all the pies we have tasted.
7. The ____________________ movie cowboy was Roy Rogers.
8. The ____________________ ingredient in the recipe is the optional cheese topping.

# Reading Comprehension

You can sequence the order of a story that you read.

Read the passage below and find out what happened in the beginning, middle, and end of the story.

## Gail's Girls

Gail has three little girls. They love to bake! They always help Gail make wonderful cakes and cupcakes at home. First, they help her take out all the ingredients. Then they help Gail mix the ingredients in a big bowl. They love to lick the spoon after mixing! After the cakes and cupcakes are finished, they all have a tea party in the backyard.

Answer the questions about the story. Write your answers on the lines below.

What did Gail's girls help her do?

What do they help her do first?

What do they help her do next?

What do they love to do after mixing the ingredients?

What do they do last?

# Addition and Subtraction

Subtracting hundreds, tens, and ones sometimes involves regrouping. If the top number in a column is less than the bottom number, you need to regroup by borrowing from the next higher place value.

Solve the equations by regrouping. Write the differences in the boxes below.

| | Hundreds | Tens | Ones |
|---|---|---|---|
| | | 3 | 16 |
| | 2 | ~~4~~ | ~~6~~ |
| − | 1 | 1 | 8 |
| | 1 | 2 | 8 |

| | Hundreds | Tens | Ones |
|---|---|---|---|
| | | | |
| | 4 | 2 | 2 |
| − | 3 | 1 | 4 |
| | | | |

| | Hundreds | Tens | Ones |
|---|---|---|---|
| | | | |
| | 5 | 1 | 3 |
| − | 4 | 3 | 5 |
| | | | |

| | Hundreds | Tens | Ones |
|---|---|---|---|
| | | | |
| | 7 | 1 | 4 |
| − | 5 | 3 | 7 |
| | | | |

| | Hundreds | Tens | Ones |
|---|---|---|---|
| | | | |
| | 2 | 9 | 5 |
| − | 1 | 2 | 7 |
| | | | |

| | Hundreds | Tens | Ones |
|---|---|---|---|
| | | | |
| | 6 | 3 | 1 |
| − | 5 | 2 | 5 |
| | | | |

| | Hundreds | Tens | Ones |
|---|---|---|---|
| | | | |
| | 8 | 1 | 3 |
| − | 3 | 0 | 5 |
| | | | |

| | Hundreds | Tens | Ones |
|---|---|---|---|
| | | | |
| | 4 | 2 | 4 |
| − | 3 | 3 | 3 |
| | | | |

| | Hundreds | Tens | Ones |
|---|---|---|---|
| | | | |
| | 6 | 1 | 3 |
| − | 2 | 7 | 6 |
| | | | |

Solve the word problem and write the problem and the answer in the box.

Olivia needs to inflate 594 balloons for her party. She takes a break after inflating 276 balloons. How many balloons does she still need to inflate?

| | Hundreds | Tens | Ones |
|---|---|---|---|
| | | | |
| − | | | |
| | | | |

# Word Relationships

**Literal meaning means that every word in a sentence conveys exactly what is being said.**

**Non-literal meaning means that some of the words or a phrase in a sentence conveys something different than what is being said.**

**Idioms are phrases that convey non-literal meanings.**

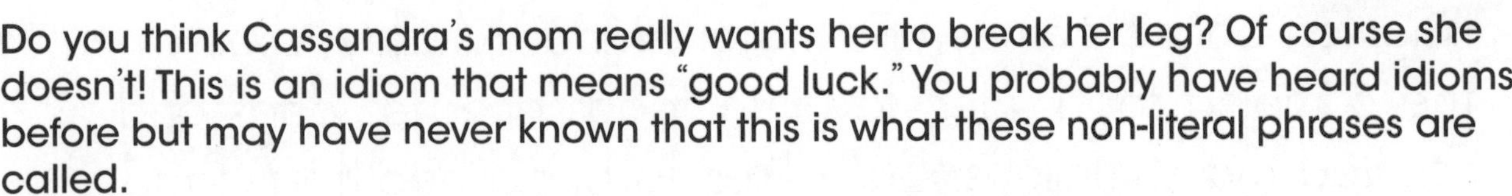

**Example:** Cassandra is about to perform her magic act. Mom whispers, "Break a leg," to Cassandra before she goes on stage.

**Do you think Cassandra's mom really wants her to break her leg? Of course she doesn't! This is an idiom that means "good luck." You probably have heard idioms before but may have never known that this is what these non-literal phrases are called.**

**Read the sentences in the left column and underline the idiom (non-literal meaning) in each sentence. In the right column, write what you think the literal meaning is that is being conveyed by the idiom.**

| Sentences with Idioms | Literal Meaning of Idioms |
|---|---|
| 1. I have butterflies in my stomach because I know the Tilt-a-Whirl will have lots of twists and turns! | This person is nervous about going on a scary ride. |
| 2. Cleaning my room will be a piece of cake because I keep it neat all of the time. | |
| 3. Mr. Andersen looks at the time and says, "It is five o'clock. I think I will call it a day." | |
| 4. "Hang in there!" Brandy shouts to Marcus as he continues to run in the marathon. | |
| 5. Sara, the babysitter, says, "I think Trevor looks a bit under the weather," to Trevor's mother. | |

# Reading Comprehension

**Read the passage below and compare and contrast the characters in the story.**

## Maddy and Lucy Go Camping

Maddy and Lucy love to go camping. Every time their mom and dad tell them they are planning a trip to the lake, they squeal with delight. For Maddy, it means time to swim and read quietly under a tree. For Lucy, it means time for board games and water skiing. Maddy loves all the camping food. Her favorite foods are hot dogs and roasted marshmallows. Lucy likes to bring healthier food from home. She eats raw carrots and granola bars when they go camping. While Maddy and Lucy both love to go camping for different reasons, they are both sad to leave the lake every time one of their camping trips comes to an end.

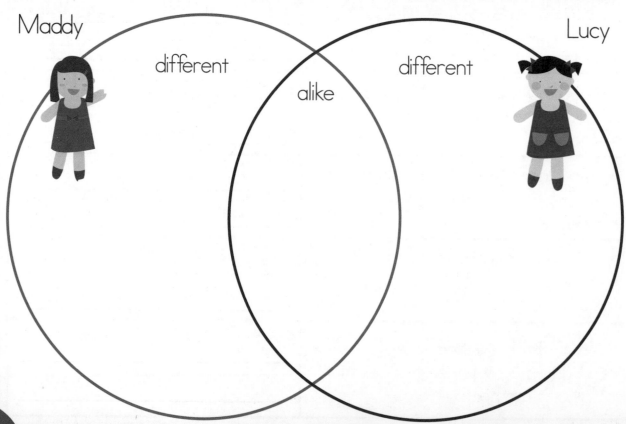

Maddy

Lucy

different

alike

different

# Fractions

Fractions are parts of a whole number. Each piece represents a part of the whole.

Example: If a cookie is cut into two equal parts, each piece is $\frac{1}{2}$ of the whole cookie.

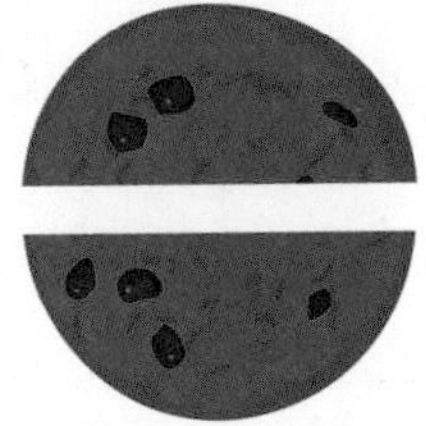

Fractions are expressed as a part over a whole. The part on top is known as the numerator. The numerator tells how many parts are shaded. The bottom number is known as the denominator. The denominator tells how many parts there are in the whole.

Example: $= \frac{1}{4}$ $\frac{\text{numerator}}{\text{denominator}}$

The 1 represents how many parts are shaded.

The 4 represents how many parts there are in the whole shape.

Write the missing numerators or denominators for the fractions shown below.

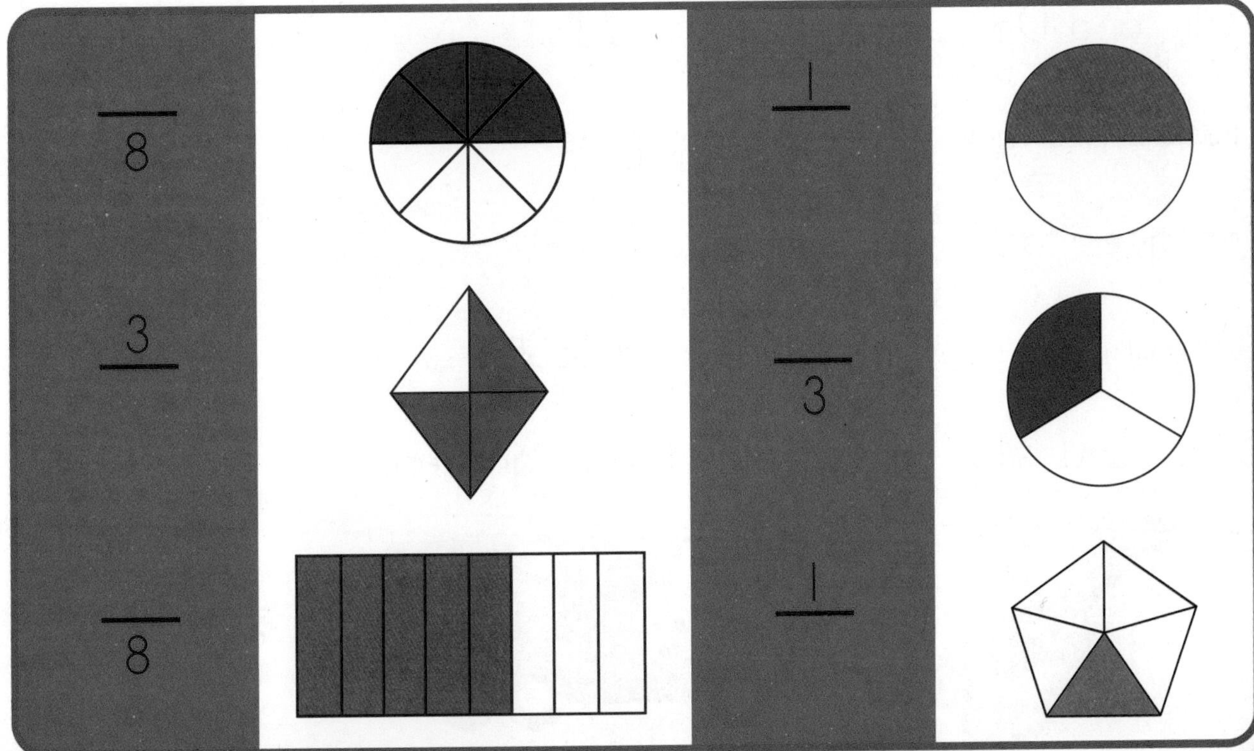

writing

# Grammar

**Every complete sentence has a subject and predicate. The subject is who or what the sentence is about. The predicate tells something about the subject.**

**Example:** Bruno likes to sing and dance.

Bruno is the subject.

Likes to sing and dance is the predicate.

**Read the sentences below. Circle the subject of each sentence and underline the predicate.**

Patty likes to count her money.

Pete learned to play guitar.

Rob is in charge of the store.

Phillip takes his daughter to the park.

Dean likes to pretend he is a fireman.

Willy and Dan play with toy trucks.

Elizabeth is always on the computer.

Ben goes for a walk every day.

Ryan and Derrick play hide and seek.

Cindy and Missy like to play in the garden.

# CERTIFICATE
## of Achievement

..............................................

has successfully completed

**LEVEL 10**

Date: ..............................

Signed: ..............................

# ANSWER KEY

Page 4

Level 1 Grade 2 Review
ABC Order
A B C D E F G H I J K L M
N O P Q R S T U V W X Y Z
1.bread
2.bride
3.butterfly
4.island
5.pumpkin
1.candy
2.car
3.cello
4.music
5.zebra


Page 5

Phonics
girl
frog
butterfly
truck
clock
kitten
lion
rake
apple
What two words above start with the same sound but different letters?
clock
kitten


Page 6

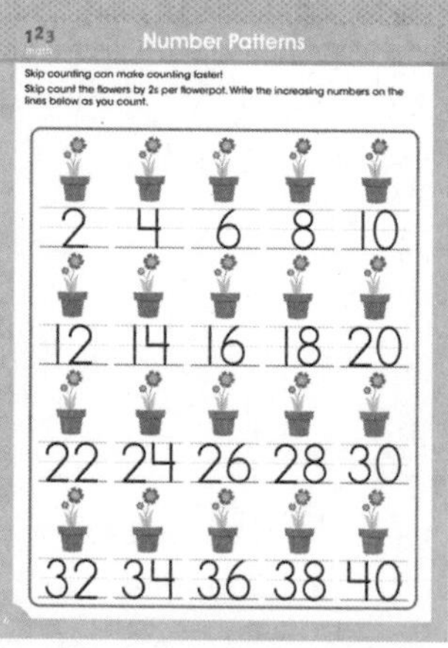


Page 7

Page 8

Page 9

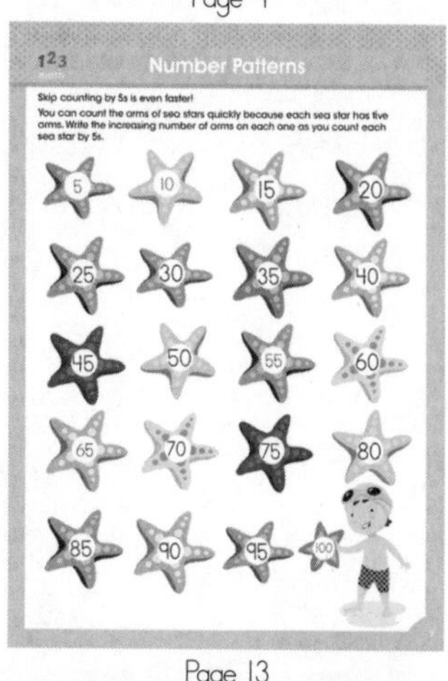


Page 10

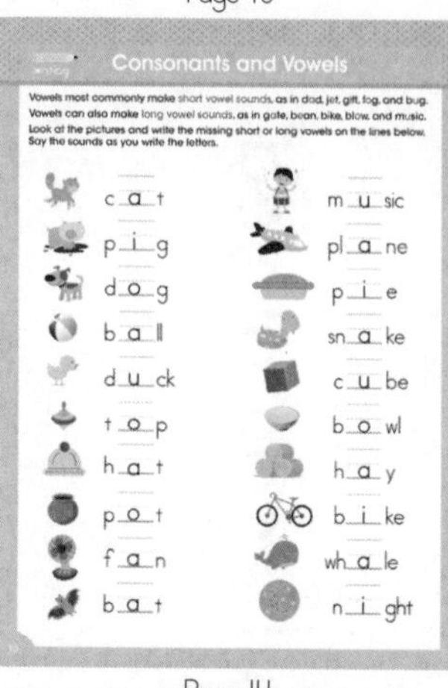


Page 11

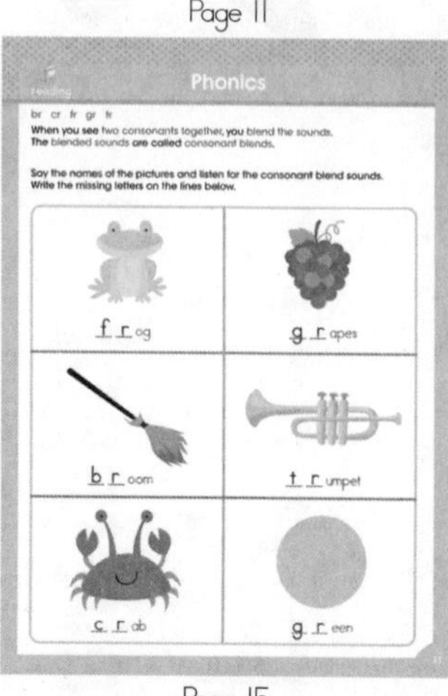


Page 12

Page 13

Page 14

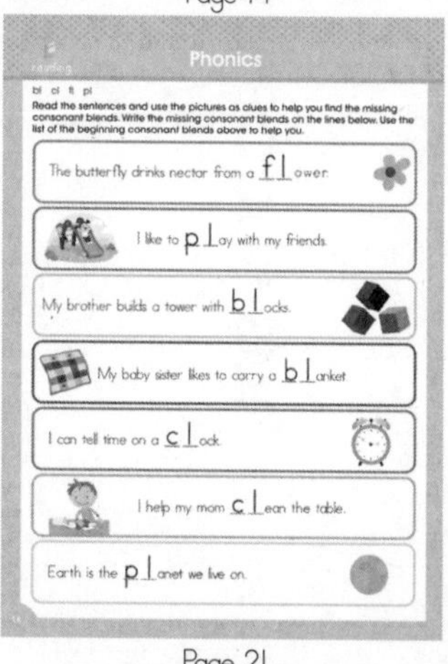

Phonics
The butterfly drinks nectar from a flower.
I like to play with my friends.
My brother builds a tower with blocks.
My baby sister likes to carry a blanket.
I can tell time on a clock.
I help my mom clean the table.
Earth is the planet we live on.


Page 15

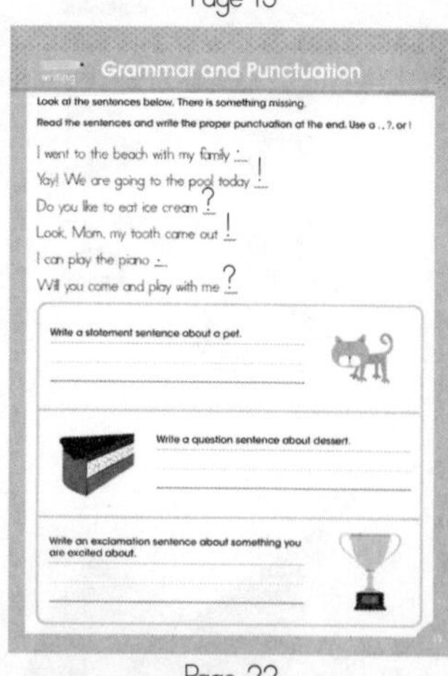


Page 19

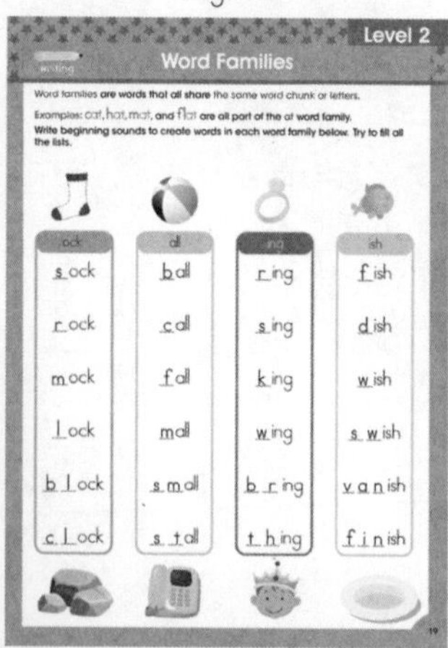


Page 20

Page 21

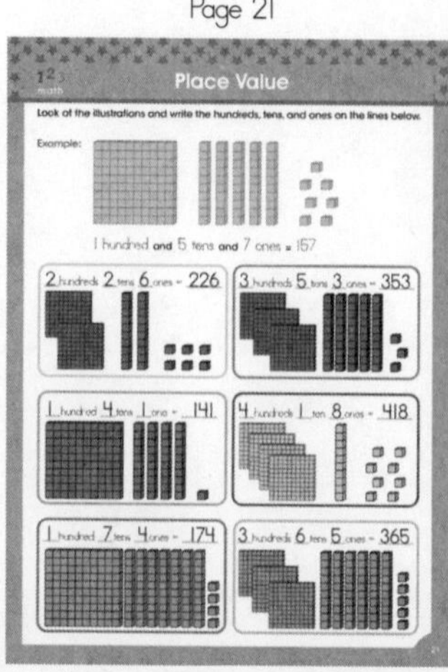


Page 22

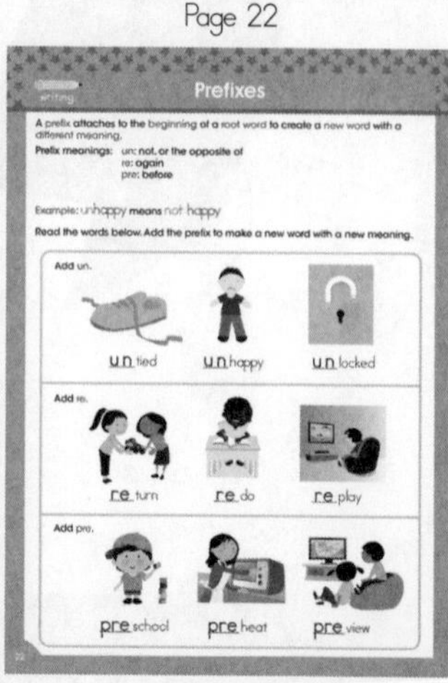

Page 23

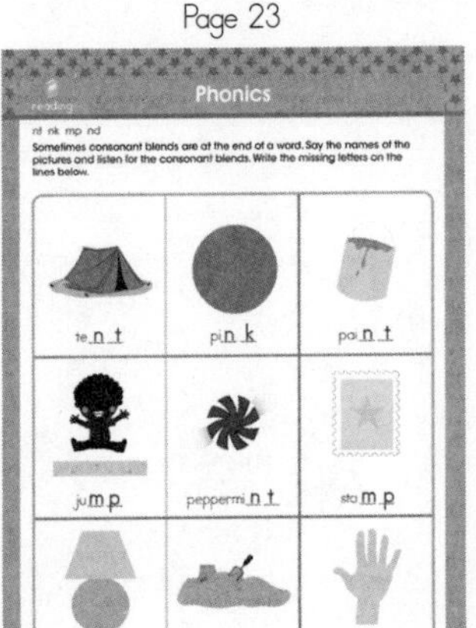


Page 24

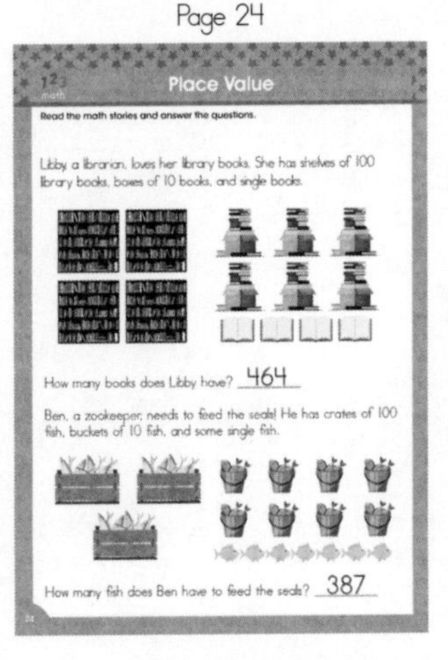


Page 25

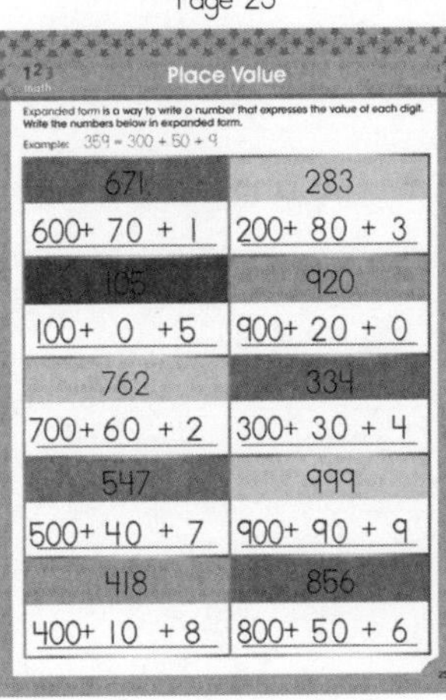

Place Value
Expanded form is a way to write a number that expresses the value of each digit. Write the numbers below in expanded form.
Example: 359 = 300 + 50 + 9
671
600+ 70 + 1
283
200+ 80 + 3
105
100+ 0 +5
920
900+ 20 + 0
762
700+ 60 + 2
334
300+ 30 + 4
547
500+ 40 + 7
999
900+ 90 + 9
418
400+ 10 + 8
856
800+ 50 + 6


Page 26

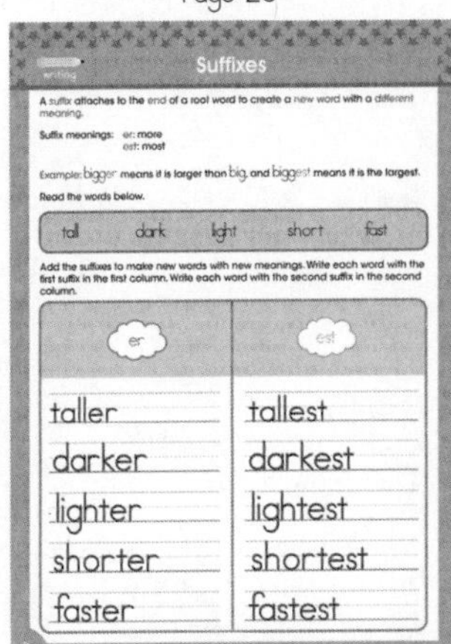


Page 27

Phonics
A digraph is a combination of two letters that make one sound. Say the names of the pictures and listen for the digraph sound. Fill in the missing digraphs for each word below.
shovel
chocolate
shore
thirty
chicken
ship
thunder
think
chilis


Page 28

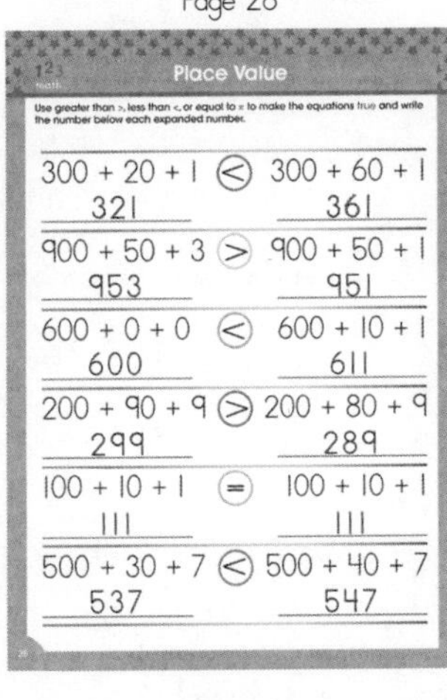

Place Value
Use greater than >, less than <, or equal to = to make the equations true and write the number below each expanded number.
300 + 20 + 1 < 300 + 60 + 1
321 361
900 + 50 + 3 > 900 + 50 + 1
953 951
600 + 0 + 0 < 600 + 10 + 1
600 611
200 + 90 + 9 > 200 + 80 + 9
299 289
100 + 10 + 1 = 100 + 10 + 1
111 111
500 + 30 + 7 < 500 + 40 + 7
537 547


Page 29

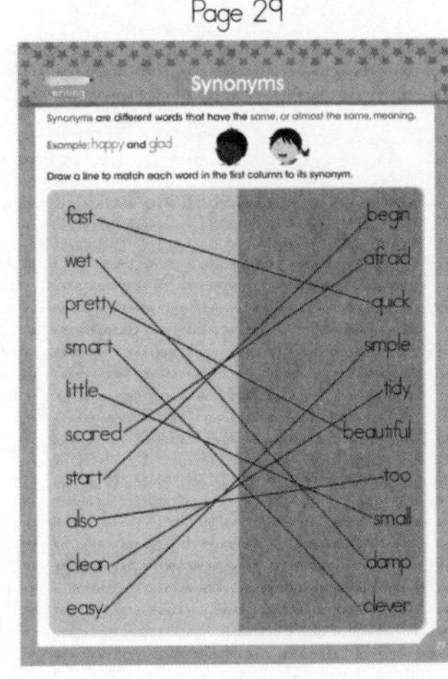

Synonyms
Synonyms are different words that have the same, or almost the same, meaning.
Example: happy and glad
Draw a line to match each word in the first column to its synonym.
fast
wet
pretty
smart
little
scared
start
also
clean
easy
begin
afraid
quick
simple
tidy
beautiful
too
small
damp
clever


Page 33

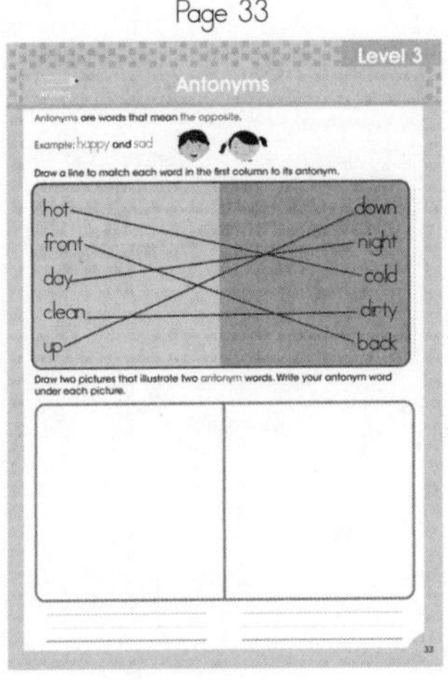

Level 3
Antonyms
Antonyms are words that mean the opposite.
Example: happy and sad
Draw a line to match each word in the first column to its antonym.
hot
front
day
clean
up
down
night
cold
dirty
back
Draw two pictures that illustrate two antonym words. Write your antonym word under each picture.


Page 34

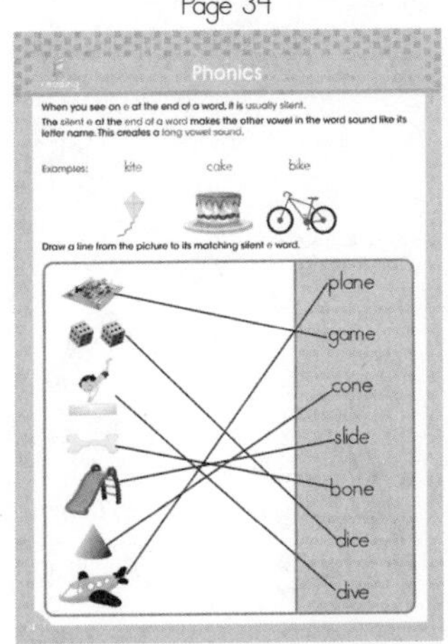


Page 35

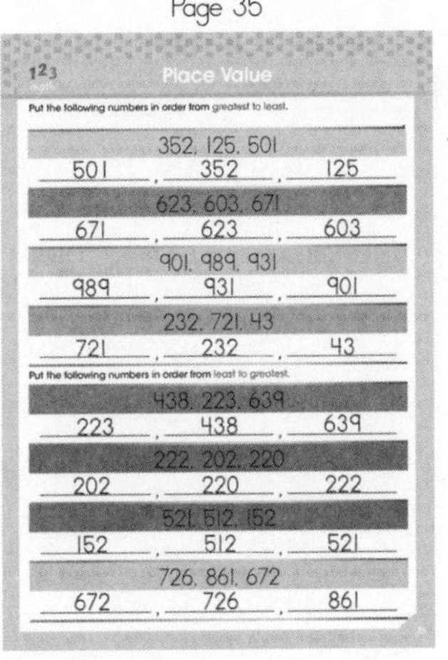

Place Value
Put the following numbers in order from greatest to least.
352, 125, 501
501 , 352 , 125
623, 603, 671
671 , 623 , 603
901, 989, 931
989 , 931 , 901
232, 721, 43
721 , 232 , 43
Put the following numbers in order from least to greatest.
438, 223, 639
223 , 438 , 639
222, 202, 220
202 , 220 , 222
521, 512, 152
152 , 512 , 521
726, 861, 672
672 , 726 , 861


Page 36

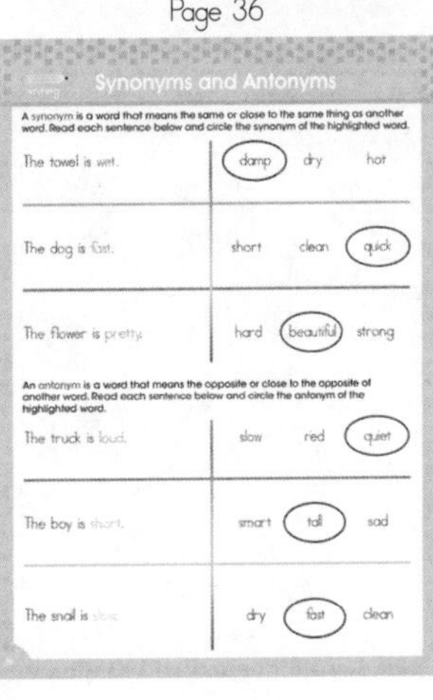


Page 37

Page 38

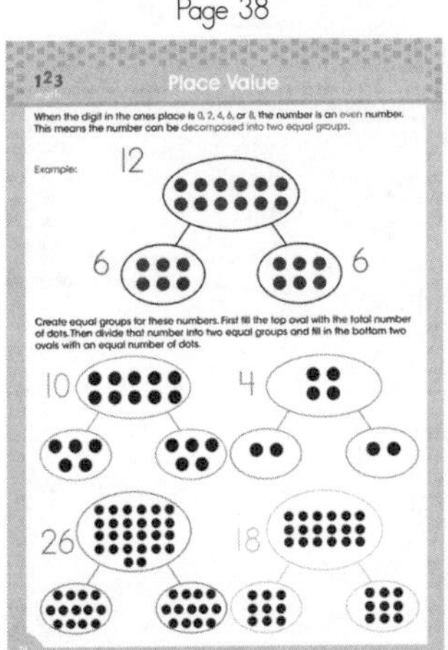


Page 39

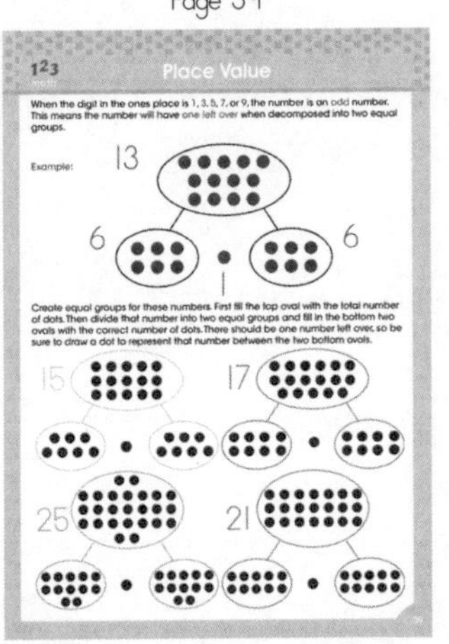


Page 40

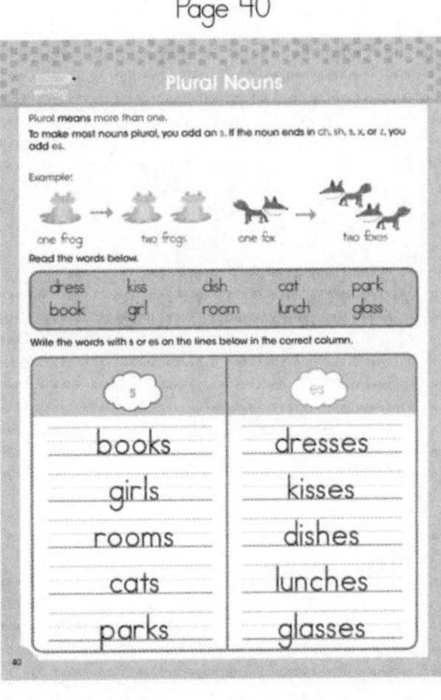


Page 41

Common Nouns
Common nouns are words for people, animals, places, and things.
horse
boy
bike
books
shoes
giraffe
Use the nouns from the pictures above to fill in the missing words in the sentences.
A giraffe has a very long neck.
The boy is wearing a blue shirt.
I ride my bike to school every day.
I fed a horse at the farm.
I learned how to tie my shoes today.
She likes to read her books.

Page 42

Phonics

The letters ee and ea both make the long e sound.

bee, queen, feet, feed, beans, eat, team, clean

Read the sentences below. Choose the correct ee or ea word from the box above to complete each sentence.

My mom asked me to clean the table.
My soccer team won the game.
I love green beans.
My favorite thing to eat is ice cream.
I feed my dog every day.
The king is married to the queen.
I am wearing shoes on my feet.
Once, I got stung by a bee.

Page 43

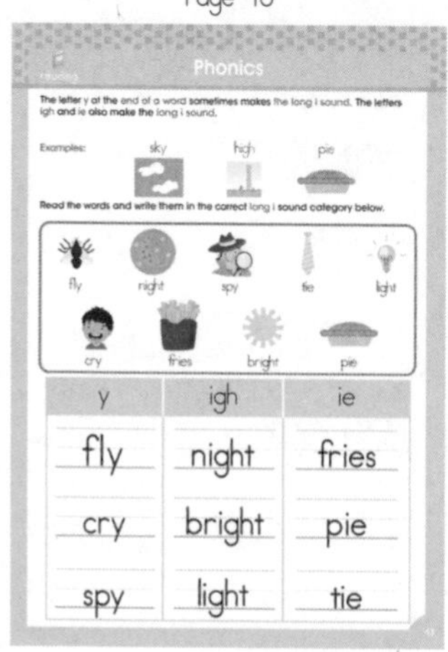
Phonics

The letter y at the end of a word sometimes makes the long i sound. The letters igh and ie also make the long i sound.

Examples: sky, high, pie

Read the words and write them in the correct long i sound category below.

fly, night, spy, tie, light, cry, fries, bright, pie

| y | igh | ie |
|---|---|---|
| fly | night | fries |
| cry | bright | pie |
| spy | light | tie |

Page 45

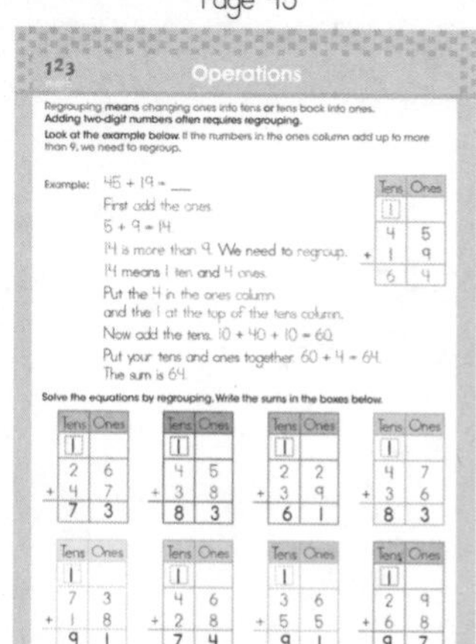
Operations

Regrouping means changing ones into tens or tens back into ones. Adding two-digit numbers often requires regrouping.

Look at the example below. If the numbers in the ones column add up to more than 9, we need to regroup.

Example: 45 + 19 = ___
First add the ones.
5 + 9 = 14
14 is more than 9. We need to regroup.
14 means 1 ten and 4 ones.
Put the 4 in the ones column and the 1 at the top of the tens column.
Now add the tens. 10 + 40 + 10 = 60
Put your tens and ones together. 60 + 4 = 64
The sum is 64.

Solve the equations by regrouping. Write the sums in the boxes below.

26 + 47 = 73; 45 + 38 = 83; 22 + 39 = 61; 47 + 36 = 83
73 + 18 = 91; 46 + 28 = 74; 36 + 55 = 91; 29 + 68 = 97

Page 48

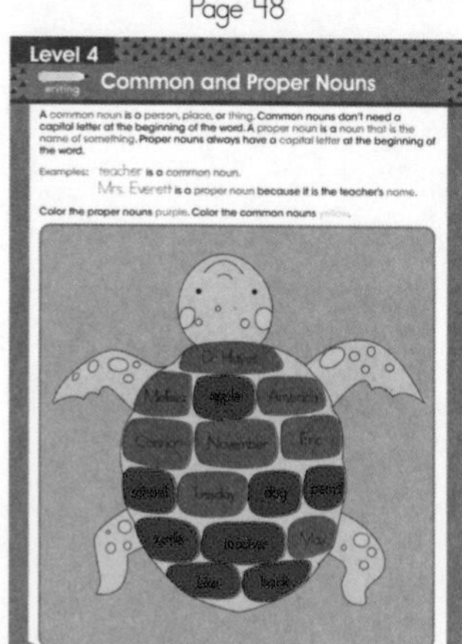
Level 4

Common and Proper Nouns

A common noun is a person, place, or thing. Common nouns don't need a capital letter at the beginning of the word. A proper noun is a noun that is the name of something. Proper nouns always have a capital letter at the beginning of the word.

Examples: teacher is a common noun.
Mrs. Everett is a proper noun because it is the teacher's name.

Color the proper nouns purple. Color the common nouns yellow.

Page 49

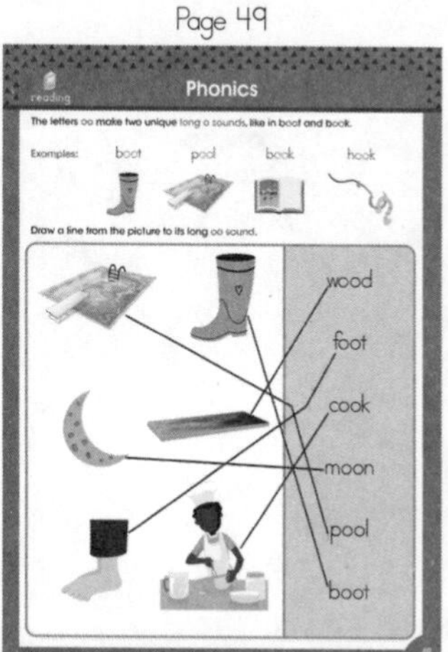
Phonics

The letters oo make two unique long o sounds, like in boot and book.

Examples: boot, pool, book, hook

Draw a line from the picture to its long oo sound.

wood, foot, cook, moon, pool, boot

Page 50

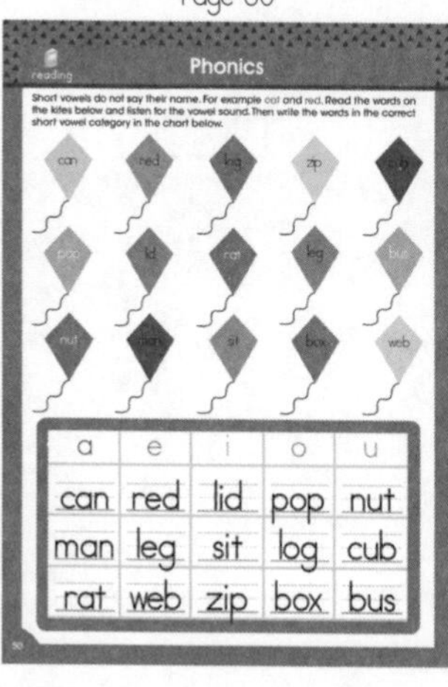
Phonics

Short vowels do not say their name. For example cat and red. Read the words on the kites below and listen for the vowel sound. Then write the words in the correct short vowel category in the chart below.

| a | e | i | o | u |
|---|---|---|---|---|
| can | red | lid | pop | nut |
| man | leg | sit | log | cub |
| rat | web | zip | box | bus |

Page 51

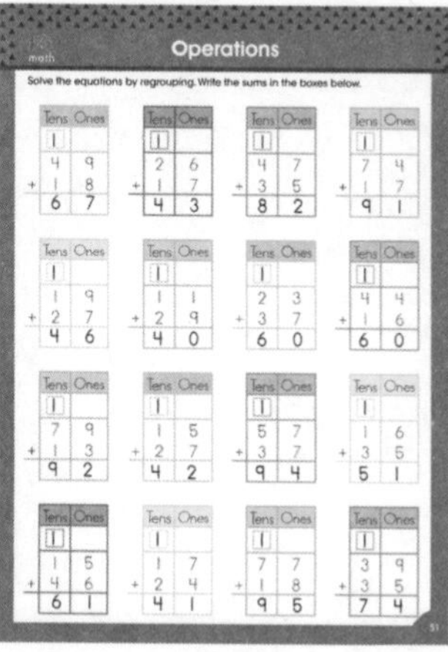
Operations

Solve the equations by regrouping. Write the sums in the boxes below.

49 + 18 = 67; 26 + 17 = 43; 47 + 35 = 82; 74 + 17 = 91
19 + 27 = 46; 11 + 29 = 40; 23 + 37 = 60; 44 + 16 = 60
79 + 13 = 92; 15 + 27 = 42; 57 + 37 = 94; 16 + 35 = 51
15 + 46 = 61; 17 + 24 = 41; 77 + 18 = 95; 39 + 35 = 74

Page 52

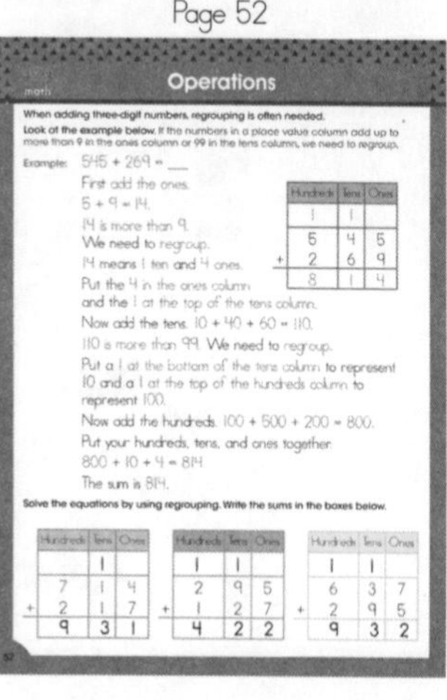
Operations

When adding three-digit numbers, regrouping is often needed.

Look at the example below. If the numbers in a place value column add up to more than 9 in the ones column or 99 in the tens column, we need to regroup.

Example: 545 + 269 = ___
First add the ones.
5 + 9 = 14.
14 is more than 9.
We need to regroup.
14 means 1 ten and 4 ones.
Put the 4 in the ones column and the 1 at the top of the tens column.
Now add the tens. 10 + 40 + 60 = 110.
110 is more than 99. We need to regroup.
Put a 1 at the bottom of the tens column to represent 10 and a 1 at the top of the hundreds column to represent 100.
Now add the hundreds. 100 + 500 + 200 = 800.
Put your hundreds, tens, and ones together.
800 + 10 + 4 = 814.
The sum is 814.

Solve the equations by using regrouping. Write the sums in the boxes below.

714 + 217 = 931; 295 + 127 = 422; 637 + 295 = 932

Page 53

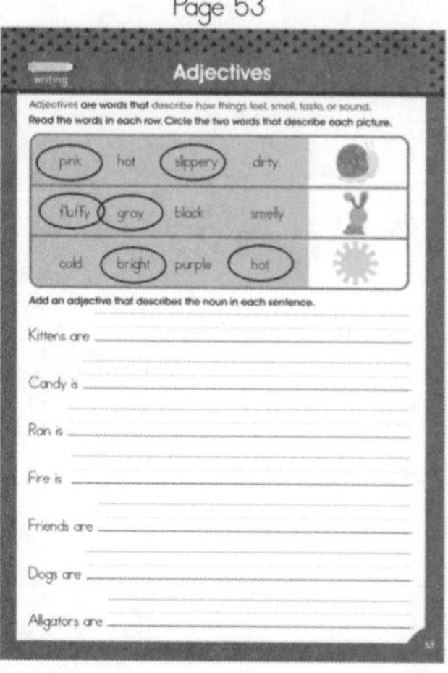
Adjectives

Adjectives are words that describe how things feel, smell, taste, or sound. Read the words in each row. Circle the two words that describe each picture.

pink, hot, slippery, dirty
fluffy, gray, black, smelly
cold, bright, purple, hot

Add an adjective that describes the noun in each sentence.

Kittens are
Candy is
Rain is
Fire is
Friends are
Dogs are
Alligators are

Page 54

Phonics

Long vowels say their name, like in go and tape. Short vowels don't say their name, like tub and bat. Read the words in the bubbles. Color the short vowel words red and the long vowel words blue.

Page 55

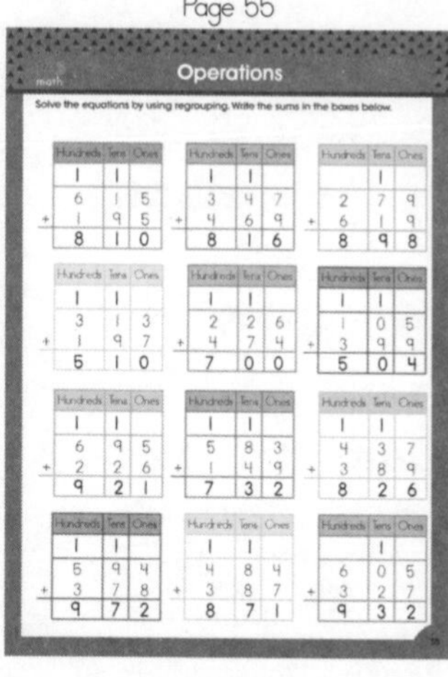
Operations

Solve the equations by using regrouping. Write the sums in the boxes below.

615 + 195 = 810; 347 + 469 = 816; 279 + 619 = 898
313 + 197 = 510; 226 + 474 = 700; 105 + 399 = 504
695 + 226 = 921; 583 + 149 = 732; 437 + 389 = 826
594 + 378 = 972; 484 + 387 = 871; 605 + 327 = 932

Page 56

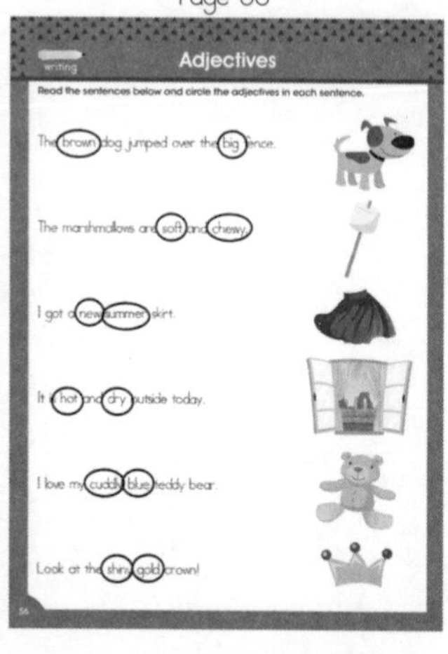
Adjectives

Read the sentences below and circle the adjectives in each sentence.

The brown dog jumped over the big fence.
The marshmallows are soft and chewy.
I got a new summer skirt.
It is hot and dry outside today.
I love my cuddly blue teddy bear.
Look at the shiny gold crown!

Page 57

Phonics

The letter c makes two sounds.
It makes a /k/ sound, like in cat.
It also makes an /s/ sound, like in face.
This is what is called a soft sound.

The letter g also makes two sounds.
It makes a /g/ sound, like in goat.
It also makes a /j/ sound, like in giraffe.
This is what is called a soft sound.

When these letters are followed by i, y, or e, they make soft sounds.

cat, face, goat, giraffe

Look at the pictures below. Circle the words that have a soft c or soft g sound.

city, mice, giant, circle, orange, goose, gem, cake, mug, game

Page 58

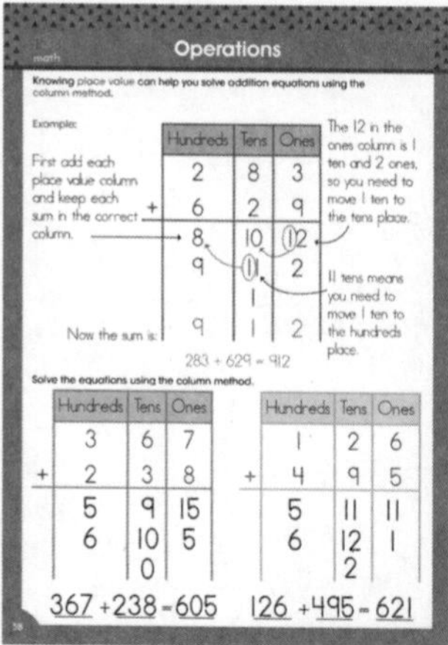
Operations

Knowing place value can help you solve addition equations using the column method.

Example:

First add each place value column and keep each sum in the correct column.

| | Hundreds | Tens | Ones |
|---|---|---|---|
| | 2 | 8 | 3 |
| + | 6 | 2 | 9 |
| | 8 | 10 | 12 |
| | 9 | 1 | 2 |

The 12 in the ones column is 1 ten and 2 ones, so you need to move 1 ten to the tens place.

11 tens means you need to move 1 ten to the hundreds place.

Now the sum is: 9 1 2

283 + 629 = 912

Solve the equations using the column method.

367 + 238 = 605; 126 + 495 = 621

Page 59

Operations

Solve the equations using the column method.

472 + 149 = 621; 128 + 375 = 503
679 + 245 = 924; 138 + 624 = 762

Page 63

Level 5

Verbs

Verbs are words that tell what a noun is doing. They are action words.



Use the picture above to help you complete the sentences. Write the words on the lines below.

The friends are throwing snowballs.
The kids are running in the snow.
The girl is swinging on the swing.
The moms are talking to each other.
The dad is drinking coffee.
The boy and girl are building a snowman.
The people are skating on the ice.

Page 65

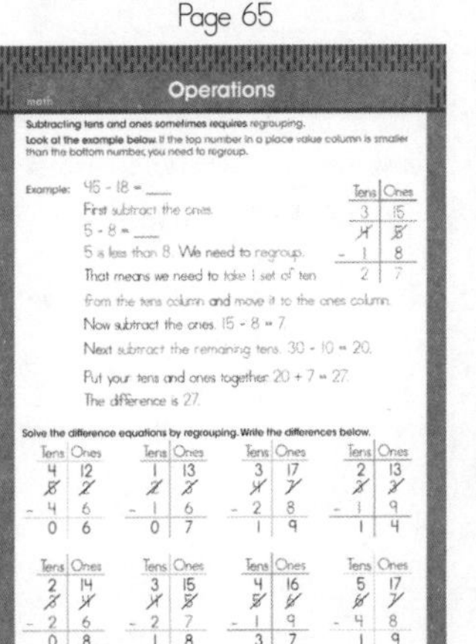
Operations

Subtracting tens and ones sometimes requires regrouping.
Look at the example below. If the top number in a place value column is smaller than the bottom number, you need to regroup.

Example: 45 - 18 = ___
First subtract the ones.
5 - 8 = ___
5 is less than 8. We need to regroup.
That means we need to take 1 set of ten from the tens column and move it to the ones column.
Now subtract the ones. 15 - 8 = 7
Next subtract the remaining tens. 30 - 10 = 20.
Put your tens and ones together: 20 + 7 = 27.
The difference is 27.

Solve the difference equations by regrouping. Write the differences below.

Page 67

Reading Comprehension

Summarizing means explaining the details of the story in just a few words. A story summary should answer these questions: who, what, when, where, and why.
Write a few words or a sentence on each line to answer the questions and summarize "Hannah's Soccer Game."

Who is the main character in the story?
Hannah.
What is happening in the story?
Hannah plays soccer, and her team plays for the championship.
When is it happening?
During the school year
Where is it happening?
On the soccer field
Why did the author write this story? What is the author's purpose?
To tell a story about Hannah and her team winning the championship. It is a story written to entertain.

Page 68

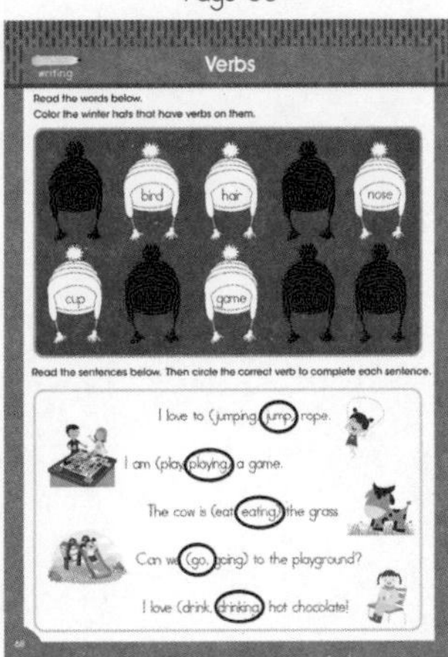
Verbs

Read the words below.
Color the winter hats that have verbs on them.
bird, hair, nose, cup, game

Read the sentences below. Then circle the correct verb to complete each sentence.
I love to (jumping, jump) rope.
I am (play, playing) a game.
The cow is (eat, eating) the grass.
Can we (go, going) to the playground?
I love (drink, drinking) hot chocolate!

Page 69

Operations

Solve the equations by regrouping. Write the differences below.

Page 71

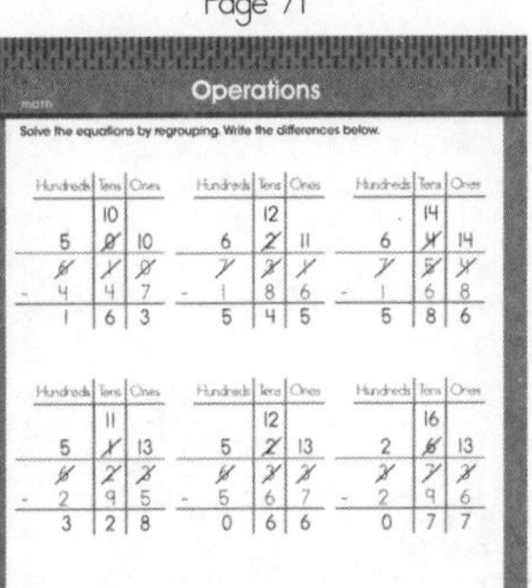
Operations

Solve the equations by regrouping. Write the differences below.

Page 73

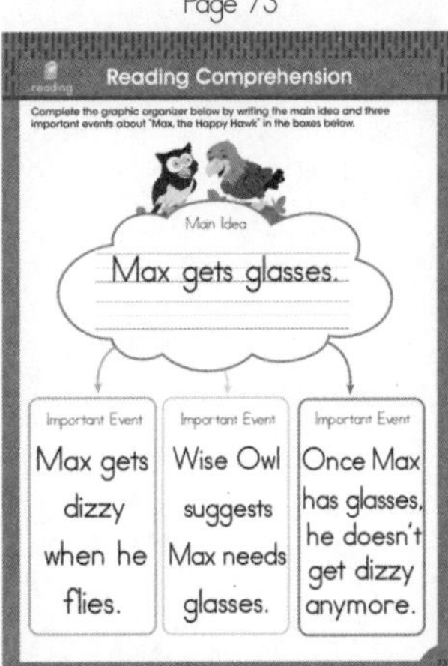
Reading Comprehension

Complete the graphic organizer below by writing the main idea and three important events about "Max, the Happy Hawk" in the boxes below.

Main Idea
Max gets glasses.

Important Event
Max gets dizzy when he flies.

Important Event
Wise Owl suggests Max needs glasses.

Important Event
Once Max has glasses, he doesn't get dizzy anymore.

Page 76

Operations

Sometimes math equations are hidden in word problems. Read each addition or subtraction word problem carefully and write an equation that shows the unknown number. Solve your equation and write the answer on the line.

Example: Ella makes bracelets for her friends and family. She had 89 but gave some away. She has 56 bracelets left. How many did she give away?
89 - ? = 56  89 - 56 = 33
Ella gave away 33 bracelets.

Oscar collects miniature race cars. He has 29 cars. His friend Caleb has 15 more cars than Oscar. How many cars does Caleb have?
29 + 15 = 44
Caleb has 44 cars.

Finn loves the space shuttle. He knows it is 122 feet long and 78 feet wide. How much longer is the space shuttle than it is wide?
122 - 78 = 44
The shuttle is 44 feet longer than it is wide.

Page 79

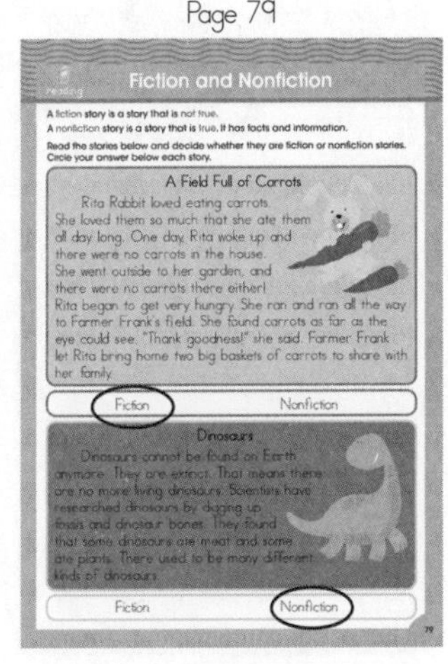
Fiction and Nonfiction

A fiction story is a story that is not true.
A nonfiction story is a story that is true. It has facts and information.
Read the stories below and decide whether they are fiction or nonfiction stories. Circle your answer below each story.

A Field Full of Carrots
Rita Rabbit loved eating carrots. She loved them so much that she ate them all day long. One day, Rita woke up and there were no carrots in the house. She went outside to her garden, and there were no carrots there either! Rita began to get very hungry. She ran and ran all the way to Farmer Frank's field. She found carrots as far as the eye could see. "Thank goodness!" she said. Farmer Frank let Rita bring home two big baskets of carrots to share with her family.
Fiction / Nonfiction

Dinosaurs
Dinosaurs cannot be found on Earth anymore. They are extinct. That means there are no more living dinosaurs. Scientists have researched dinosaurs by digging up fossils and dinosaur bones. They found that some dinosaurs ate meat and some ate plants. There used to be many different kinds of dinosaurs.
Fiction / Nonfiction

Page 80

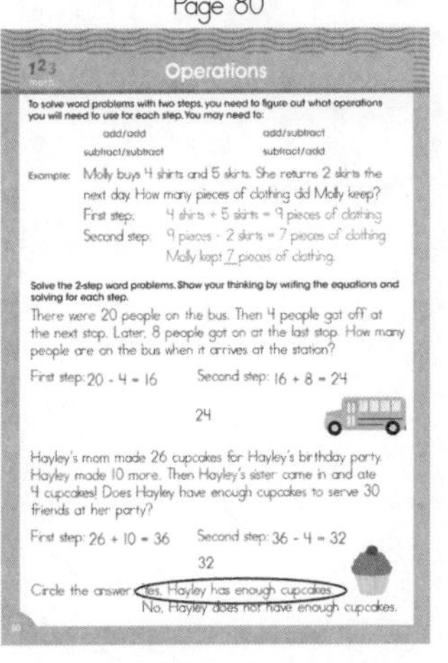
Operations

To solve word problems with two steps, you will need to figure out what operations you will need to use for each step. You may need to:
add/add  add/subtract
subtract/subtract  subtract/add

Example: Molly buys 4 shirts and 5 skirts. She returns 2 skirts the next day. How many pieces of clothing did Molly keep?
First step: 4 shirts + 5 skirts = 9 pieces of clothing
Second step: 9 pieces - 2 skirts = 7 pieces of clothing
Molly kept 7 pieces of clothing.

Solve the 2-step word problems. Show your thinking by writing the equations and solving for each step.

There were 20 people on the bus. Then 4 people got off at the next stop. Later, 8 people got on at the last stop. How many people are on the bus when it arrives at the station?
First step: 20 - 4 = 16  Second step: 16 + 8 = 24
24

Hayley's mom made 26 cupcakes for Hayley's birthday party. Hayley made 10 more. Then Hayley's sister came in and ate 4 cupcakes! Does Hayley have enough cupcakes to serve 30 friends at her party?
First step: 26 + 10 = 36  Second step: 36 - 4 = 32
32
Circle the answer: Yes, Hayley has enough cupcakes.
No, Hayley does not have enough cupcakes.

Page 81

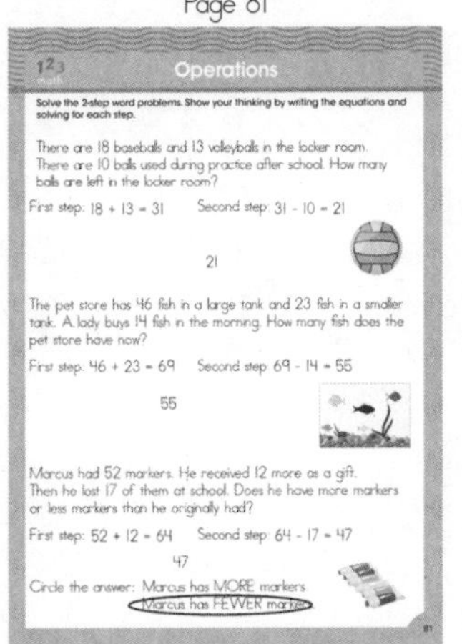
Operations

Solve the 2-step word problems. Show your thinking by writing the equations and solving for each step.

There are 18 baseballs and 13 volleyballs in the locker room. There are 10 balls used during practice after school. How many balls are left in the locker room?
First step: 18 + 13 = 31  Second step: 31 - 10 = 21
21

The pet store has 46 fish in a large tank and 23 fish in a smaller tank. A lady buys 14 fish in the morning. How many fish does the pet store have now?
First step: 46 + 23 = 69  Second step: 69 - 14 = 55
55

Marcus had 52 markers. He received 12 more as a gift. Then he lost 17 of them at school. Does he have more markers or less markers than he originally had?
First step: 52 + 12 = 64  Second step: 64 - 17 = 47
47
Circle the answer: Marcus has MORE markers.
Marcus has FEWER markers.

Page 82

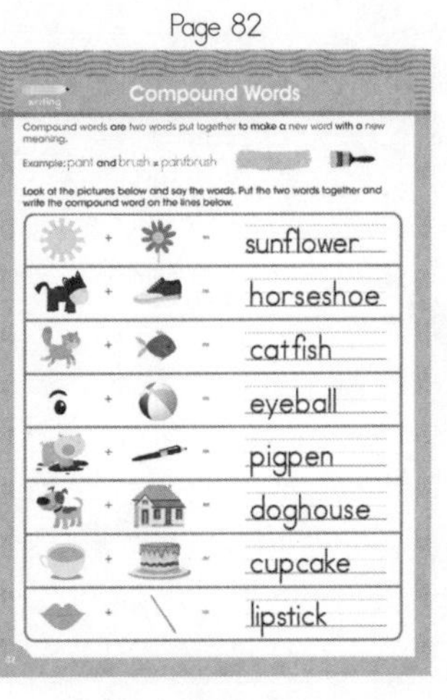
Compound Words

Compound words are two words put together to make a new word with a new meaning.
Example: paint and brush = paintbrush

Look at the pictures below and say the words. Put the two words together and write the compound word on the lines below.
sunflower
horseshoe
catfish
eyeball
pigpen
doghouse
cupcake
lipstick

Page 83

Nonfiction

The table of contents tells readers which topics can be found in a book and the pages where they can be found.

Horses
Table of Contents
What Horses Eat 2
Where Horses Live 4
Horse Babies 6
Horse Facts 8

Use the table of contents above to answer the questions. Write your answers on the lines below.
How many topics are in the book?
Four
Which topic begins on page 4?
Where Horses Live
Which topic begins on page 6?
Horse Babies
If I want to find out what horses eat, what topic will help me learn this information?
What Horses Eat

Page 84

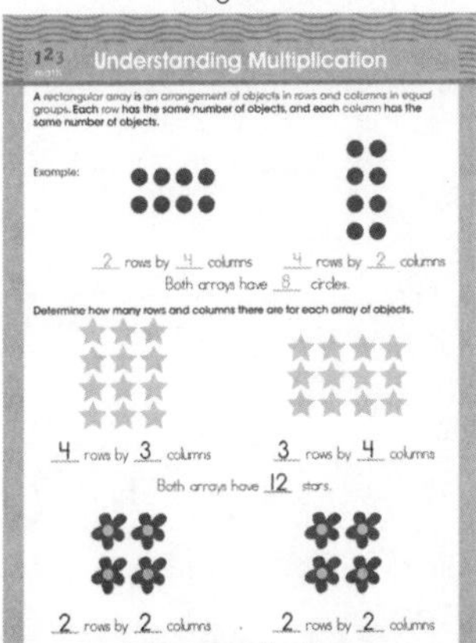
Understanding Multiplication

A rectangular array is an arrangement of objects in rows and columns in equal groups. Each row has the same number of objects, and each column has the same number of objects.

Example:
2 rows by 4 columns  4 rows by 2 columns
Both arrays have 8 circles.

Determine how many rows and columns there are for each array of objects.
4 rows by 3 columns  3 rows by 4 columns
Both arrays have 12 stars.
2 rows by 2 columns  2 rows by 2 columns
Both arrays have 4 flowers.

Page 85

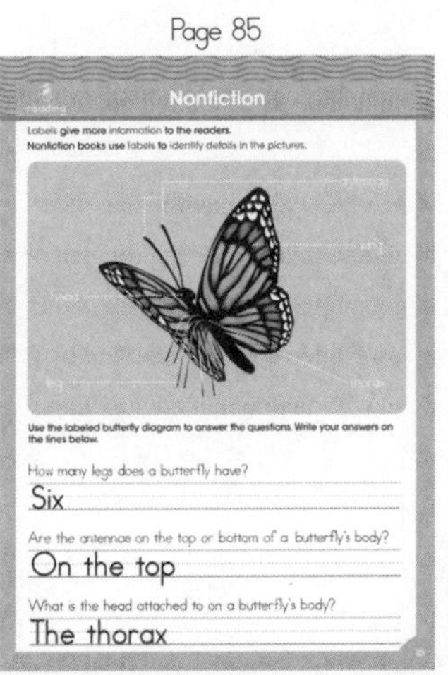
Nonfiction

Labels give more information to the readers.
Nonfiction books use labels to identify details in the pictures.

Use the labeled butterfly diagram to answer the questions. Write your answers on the lines below.
How many legs does a butterfly have?
Six
Are the antennae on the top or bottom of a butterfly's body?
On the top
What is the head attached to on a butterfly's body?
The thorax

Page 86

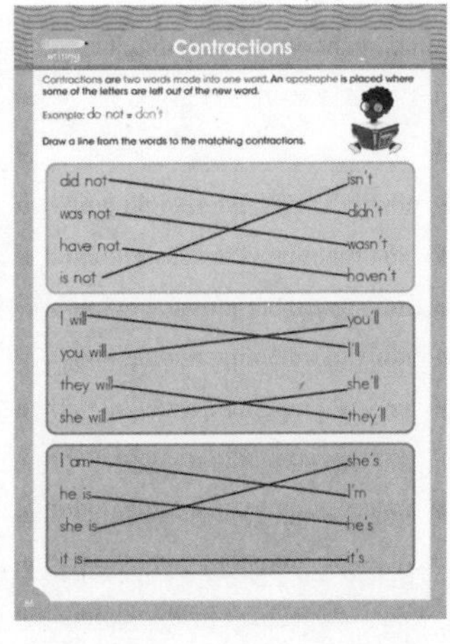
Contractions

Contractions are two words made into one word. An apostrophe is placed where some of the letters are left out of the new word.
Example: do not = don't

Draw a line from the words to the matching contractions.
did not — didn't
was not — wasn't
have not — haven't
is not — isn't
I will — I'll
you will — you'll
they will — they'll
she will — she'll
I am — I'm
he is — he's
she is — she's
it is — it's

Page 87

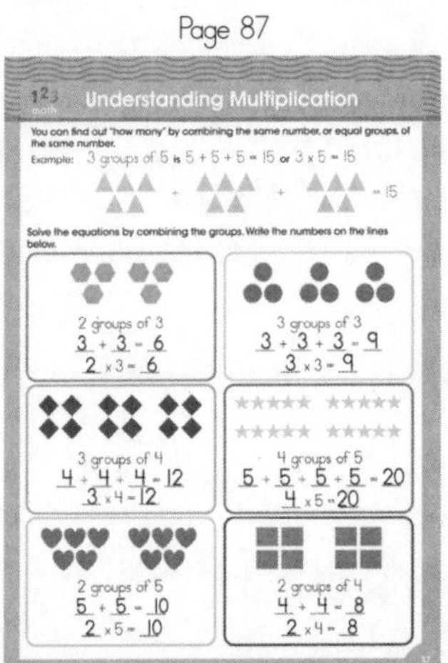
Understanding Multiplication

You can find out "how many" by combining the same number, or equal groups, of the same number.
Example: 3 groups of 5 is 5 + 5 + 5 = 15 or 3 x 5 = 15

Solve the equations by combining the groups. Write the numbers on the lines below.
2 groups of 3
3 + 3 = 6
2 x 3 = 6
3 groups of 3
3 + 3 + 3 = 9
3 x 3 = 9
3 groups of 4
4 + 4 + 4 = 12
3 x 4 = 12
4 groups of 5
5 + 5 + 5 + 5 = 20
4 x 5 = 20
2 groups of 5
5 + 5 = 10
2 x 5 = 10
2 groups of 4
4 + 4 = 8
2 x 4 = 8

Page 90

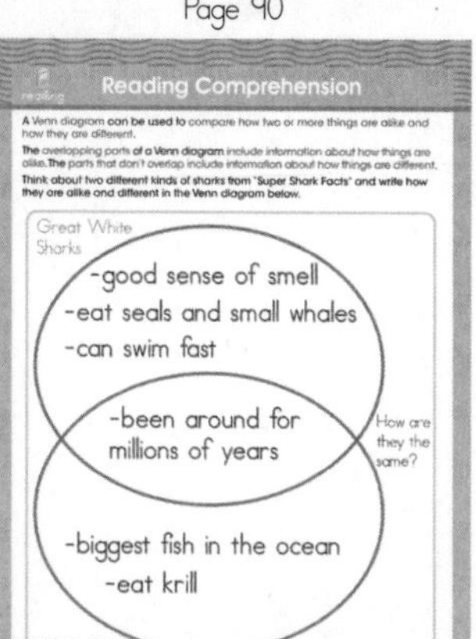
Reading Comprehension

A Venn diagram can be used to compare how two or more things are alike and how they are different.

The overlapping parts of a Venn diagram include information about how things are alike. The parts that don't overlap include information about how things are different.

Think about two different kinds of sharks from "Super Shark Facts" and write how they are alike and different in the Venn diagram below.

Great White Sharks
-good sense of smell
-eat seals and small whales
-can swim fast
-been around for millions of years
How are they the same?
-biggest fish in the ocean
-eat krill
Whale Sharks

Page 93

Contractions — Level 7

A contraction is when two words are combined with an apostrophe. Read the two words in each box and write their contraction on the lines below. Then color the animals.

did not — didn't; was not — wasn't; have not — haven't
is not — isn't; I am — I'm; he is — he's
she is — she's; it is — it's; I will — I'll
you will — you'll; they will — they'll; she will — she'll

Page 94

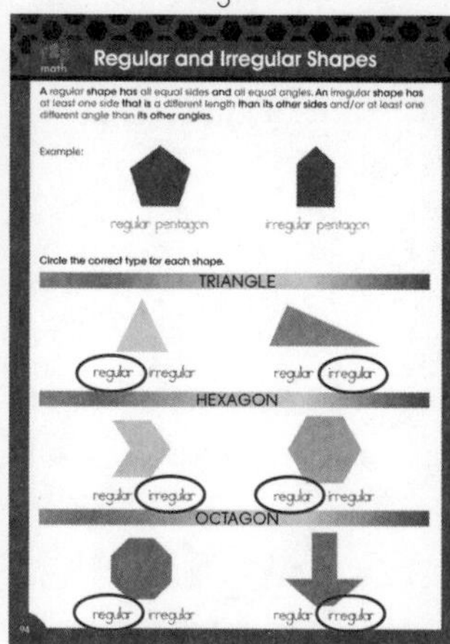
Regular and Irregular Shapes

A regular shape has all equal sides and all equal angles. An irregular shape has at least one side that is a different length than its other sides and/or at least one different angle than its other angles.

Example: regular pentagon, irregular pentagon

Circle the correct type for each shape.

TRIANGLE: regular irregular; regular irregular
HEXAGON: regular irregular; regular irregular
OCTAGON: regular irregular; regular irregular

Page 95

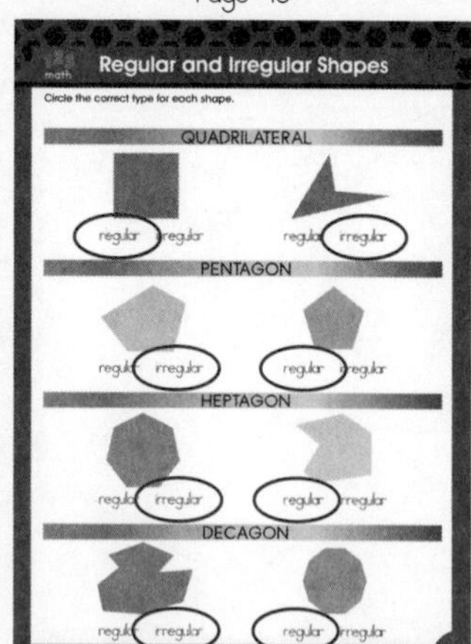
Regular and Irregular Shapes

Circle the correct type for each shape.

QUADRILATERAL: regular irregular; regular irregular
PENTAGON: regular irregular; regular irregular
HEPTAGON: regular irregular; regular irregular
DECAGON: regular irregular; regular irregular

Page 96

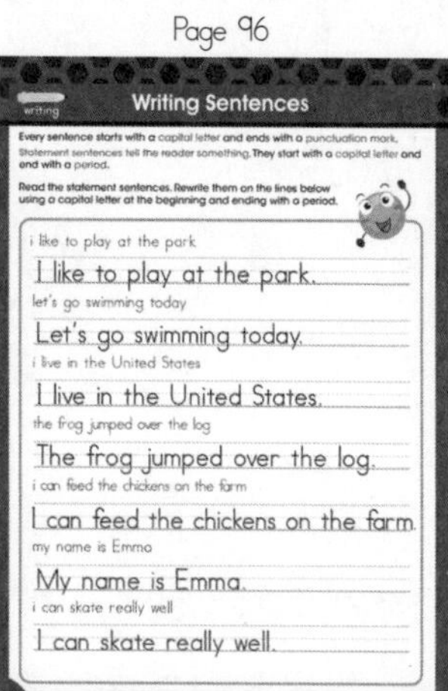
Writing Sentences

Every sentence starts with a capital letter and ends with a punctuation mark. Statement sentences tell the reader something. They start with a capital letter and end with a period.

Read the statement sentences. Rewrite them on the lines below using a capital letter at the beginning and ending with a period.

i like to play at the park — I like to play at the park.
let's go swimming today — Let's go swimming today.
i live in the United States — I live in the United States.
the frog jumped over the log — The frog jumped over the log.
i can feed the chickens on the farm — I can feed the chickens on the farm.
my name is Emma — My name is Emma.
i can skate really well — I can skate really well.

Page 97

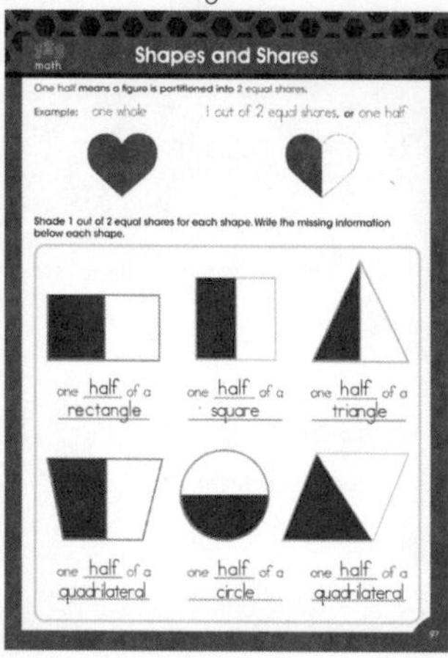
Shapes and Shares

One half means a figure is partitioned into 2 equal shares.

Example: one whole; 1 out of 2 equal shares, or one half

Shade 1 out of 2 equal shares for each shape. Write the missing information below each shape.

one half of a rectangle; one half of a square; one half of a triangle
one half of a quadrilateral; one half of a circle; one half of a quadrilateral

Page 100

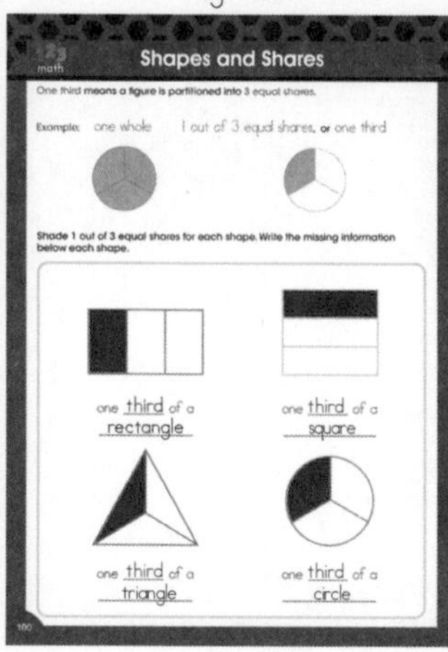
Shapes and Shares

One third means a figure is partitioned into 3 equal shares.

Example: one whole; 1 out of 3 equal shares, or one third

Shade 1 out of 3 equal shares for each shape. Write the missing information below each shape.

one third of a rectangle; one third of a square
one third of a triangle; one third of a circle

Page 101

Nonfiction

Nonfiction text often has photographs and realistic illustrations. They are meant to give the reader a realistic idea of what things actually look like.

Sometimes the pictures or illustrations have captions that provide more information about the picture or illustration.

Use the illustration and caption to answer the questions below.

What do you see in the illustration?
Trees, grass, flowers, rocks, and butterflies
What does the caption tell you about the illustration?
Butterflies need to live near a water source.

Page 102

Writing Sentences

Question sentences ask the reader a question. They start with a capital letter and end with a question mark.

Read the question sentences. Rewrite them on the lines below using a capital letter at the beginning and ending with a question mark.

what is your favorite sport — What is your favorite sport?
do you know how to tie your shoes — Do you know how to tie your shoes?
can you come out to play today — Can you come out to play today?
what is your favorite color — What is your favorite color?
what grade are you in — What grade are you in?
who is your best friend — Who is your best friend?
where do you live — Where do you live?

Page 103

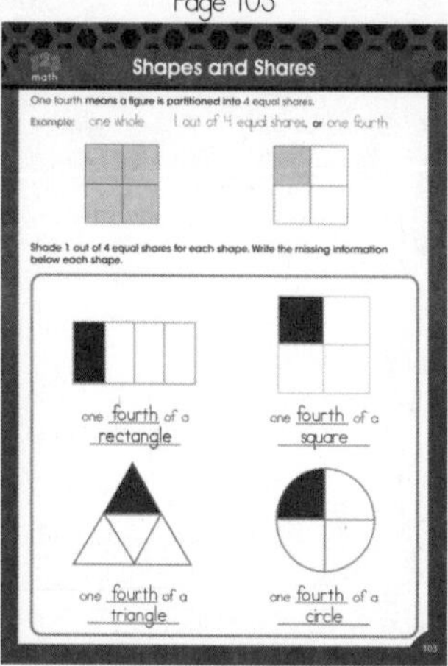
Shapes and Shares

One fourth means a figure is partitioned into 4 equal shares.

Example: one whole; 1 out of 4 equal shares, or one fourth

Shade 1 out of 4 equal shares for each shape. Write the missing information below each shape.

one fourth of a rectangle; one fourth of a square
one fourth of a triangle; one fourth of a circle

Page 109

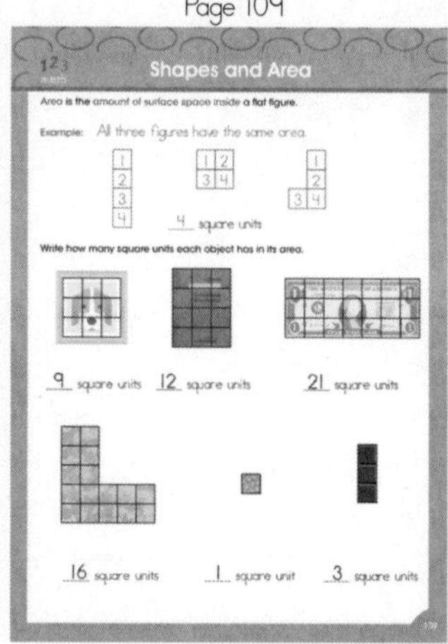
Shapes and Area

Area is the amount of surface space inside a flat figure.

Example: All three figures have the same area. 4 square units

Write how many square units each object has in its area.

9 square units; 12 square units; 21 square units
16 square units; 1 square unit; 3 square units

Page 110

Writing Sentences

Exclamation sentences tell the reader about something that is exciting, scary, or surprising. They start with a capital letter and end with an exclamation mark. Commands are short sentences with only a noun and verb. Commands also start with a capital letter and end with an exclamation mark.

Read the sentences. Rewrite them on the lines below using a capital letter at the beginning and ending with an exclamation mark.

look at that scary monster — Look at that scary monster!
i won the race — I won the race!
look at the beautiful fireworks — Look at the beautiful fireworks!
sit down — Sit down!
go, team — Go, team!
it is my birthday today — It is my birthday today!
look out — Look out!

Page 111

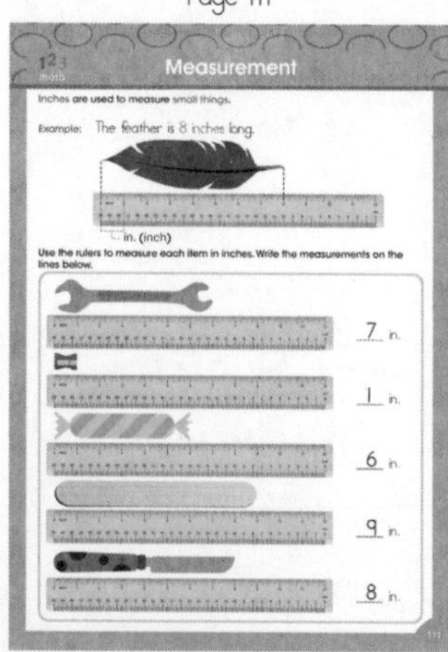
Measurement

Inches are used to measure small things.

Example: The feather is 8 inches long. in. (inch)

Use the rulers to measure each item in inches. Write the measurements on the lines below.

7 in.; 1 in.; 6 in.; 9 in.; 8 in.

Page 112

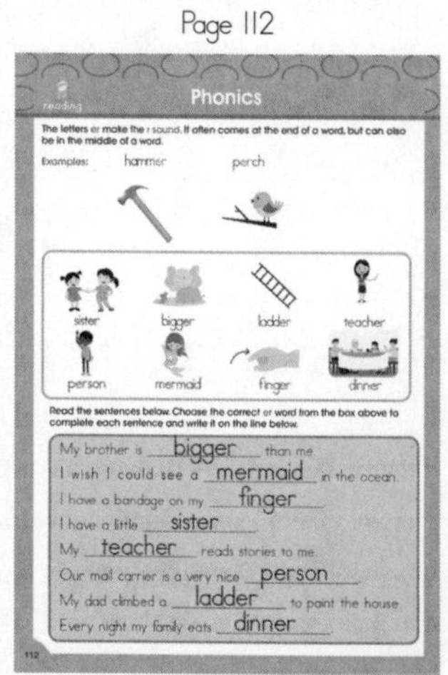
Phonics

The letters er make the r sound. It often comes at the end of a word, but can also be in the middle of a word.

Examples: hammer, perch

sister, bigger, ladder, teacher, person, mermaid, finger, dinner

Read the sentences below. Choose the correct er word from the box above to complete each sentence and write it on the line below.

My brother is bigger than me.
I wish I could see a mermaid in the ocean.
I have a bandage on my finger.
I have a little sister.
My teacher reads stories to me.
Our mail carrier is a very nice person.
My dad climbed a ladder to paint the house.
Every night my family eats dinner.

Page 113

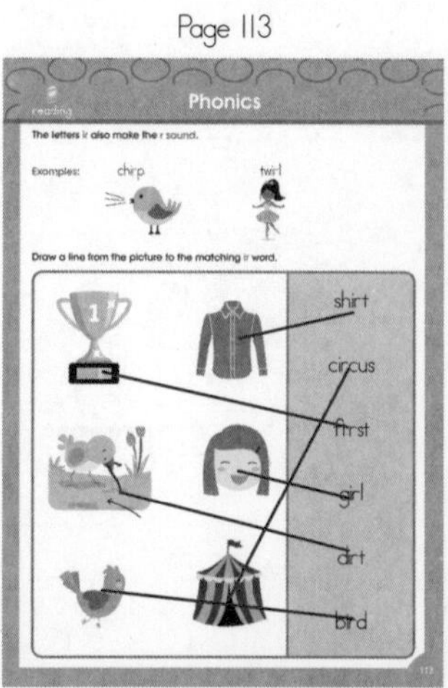
Phonics

The letters ir also make the r sound.

Examples: chirp, twirl

Draw a line from the picture to the matching ir word.

shirt, circus, first, girl, dirt, bird

Page 116

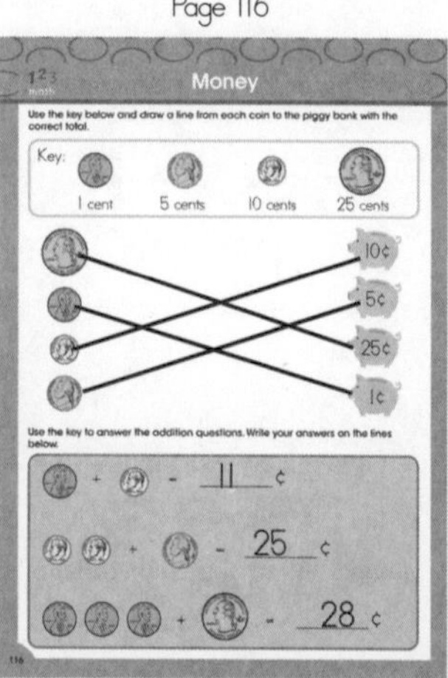
Money

Use the key below and draw a line from each coin to the piggy bank with the correct total.

Key: 1 cent, 5 cents, 10 cents, 25 cents

10¢, 5¢, 25¢, 1¢

Use the key to answer the addition questions. Write your answers on the lines below.

11 ¢
25 ¢
28 ¢

Page 117

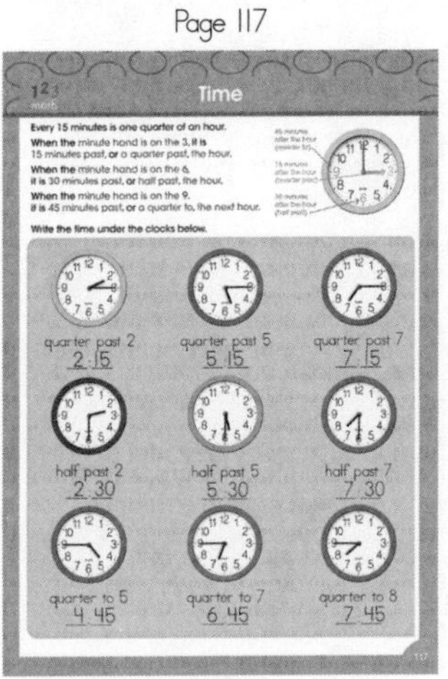
## Time

Every 15 minutes is one quarter of an hour.
When the minute hand is on the 3, it is 15 minutes past, or a quarter past, the hour.
When the minute hand is on the 6, it is 30 minutes past, or half past, the hour.
When the minute hand is on the 9, it is 45 minutes past, or a quarter to, the next hour.

Write the time under the clocks below.

quarter past 2 2:15 — quarter past 5 5:15 — quarter past 7 7:15
half past 2 2:30 — half past 5 5:30 — half past 7 7:30
quarter to 5 4:45 — quarter to 7 6:45 — quarter to 8 7:45

Page 119

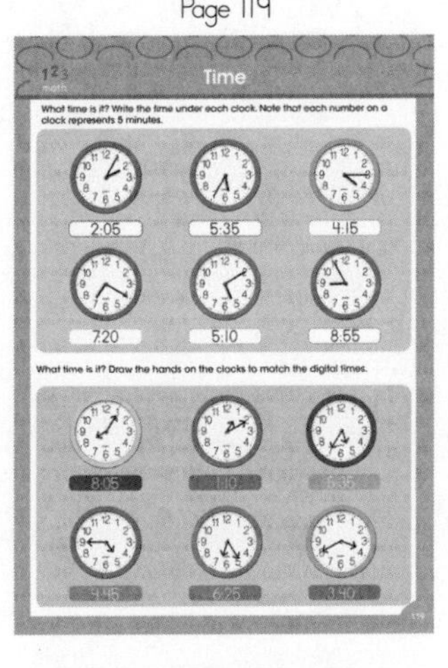
## Time

What time is it? Write the time under each clock. Note that each number on a clock represents 5 minutes.

2:05 — 5:35 — 4:15
7:20 — 5:10 — 8:55

What time is it? Draw the hands on the clocks to match the digital times.

8:05 — 1:10 — 6:35
3:45 — 6:25 — 3:40

Page 120

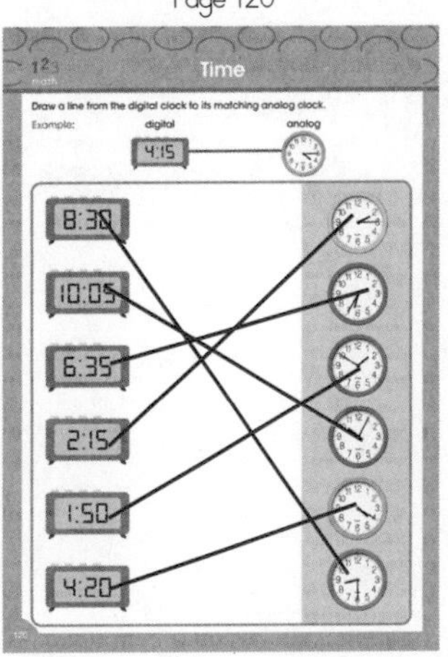
## Time

Draw a line from the digital clock to its matching analog clock.

Example: digital 4:15 — analog

8:30 — 10:05 — 6:35 — 2:15 — 1:50 — 4:20

Page 121

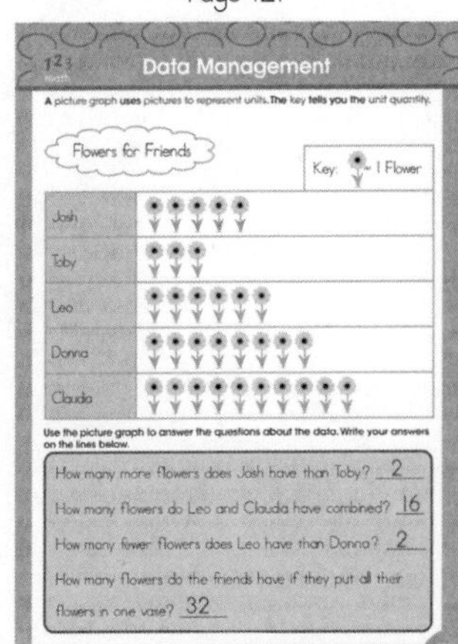
## Data Management

A picture graph uses pictures to represent units. The key tells you the unit quantity.

Flowers for Friends — Key: 1 Flower

Josh, Toby, Leo, Donna, Claudia

Use the picture graph to answer the questions about the data. Write your answers on the lines below.

How many more flowers does Josh have than Toby? 2
How many flowers do Leo and Claudia have combined? 16
How many fewer flowers does Leo have than Donna? 2
How many flowers do the friends have if they put all their flowers in one vase? 32

Page 123

## Level 9 Grade 3 Foundations
## ABC Order

Putting words into ABC order means they are in the order of the alphabet. If there are multiple words with the same first letter, you need to look at the second letter and sometimes the third letter to put the words in the correct alphabetical order.

Example: diamond dog doughnut

Put all the words in ABC order. Then rewrite them all in order on the lines below.

apple, apron, astronaut, pole, pond, porcupine, sea star, shark, shell, table, turtle, tusks

Page 124

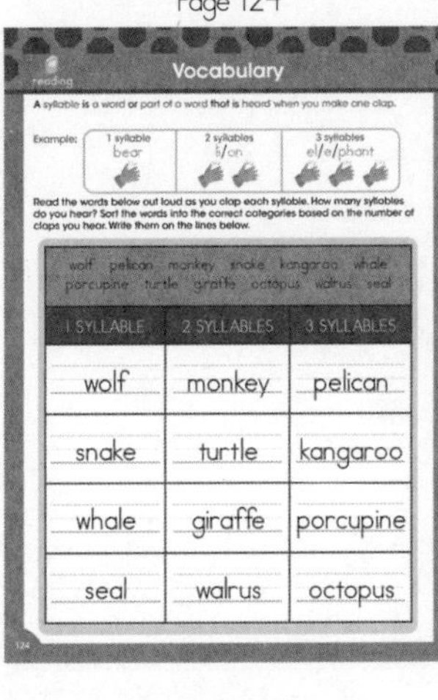
## Vocabulary

A syllable is a word or part of a word that is heard when you make one clap.

Read the words below out loud as you clap each syllable. How many syllables do you hear? Sort the words into the correct categories based on the number of claps you hear. Write them on the lines below.

| 1 SYLLABLE | 2 SYLLABLES | 3 SYLLABLES |
|---|---|---|
| wolf | monkey | pelican |
| snake | turtle | kangaroo |
| whale | giraffe | porcupine |
| seal | walrus | octopus |

Page 125

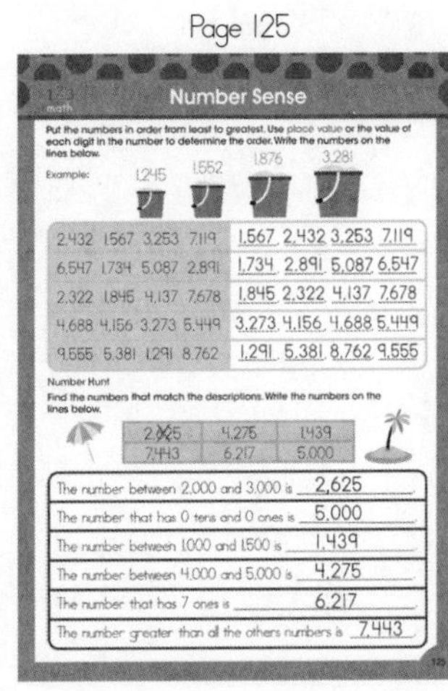
## Number Sense

Put the numbers in order from least to greatest.

| | |
|---|---|
| 2,432 1,567 3,253 7,119 | 1,567 2,432 3,253 7,119 |
| 6,547 1,734 5,087 2,891 | 1,734 2,891 5,087 6,547 |
| 2,322 1,845 4,137 7,678 | 1,845 2,322 4,137 7,678 |
| 4,688 4,156 3,273 5,449 | 3,273 4,156 4,688 5,449 |
| 9,555 5,381 1,291 8,762 | 1,291 5,381 8,762 9,555 |

Number Hunt

The number between 2,000 and 3,000 is 2,625
The number that has 0 tens and 0 ones is 5,000
The number between 1,000 and 1,500 is 1,439
The number between 4,000 and 5,000 is 4,275
The number that has 7 ones is 6,217
The number greater than all the others numbers is 7,443

Page 126

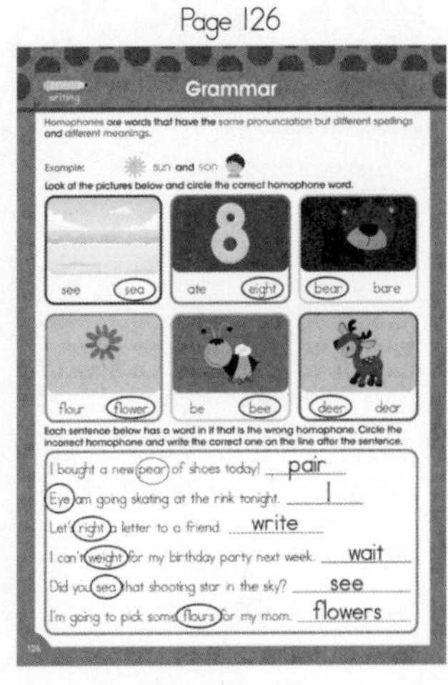
## Grammar

Homophones are words that have the same pronunciation but different spellings and different meanings.

Example: sun and son

see sea — ate eight — bear bare — flour flower — be bee — deer dear

I bought a new pear of shoes today! pair
Eye am going skating at the rink tonight. I
Let right a letter to a friend. write
I can't weight for my birthday party next week. wait
Did you sea that shooting star in the sky? see
I'm going to pick some flours for my mom. flowers

Page 127

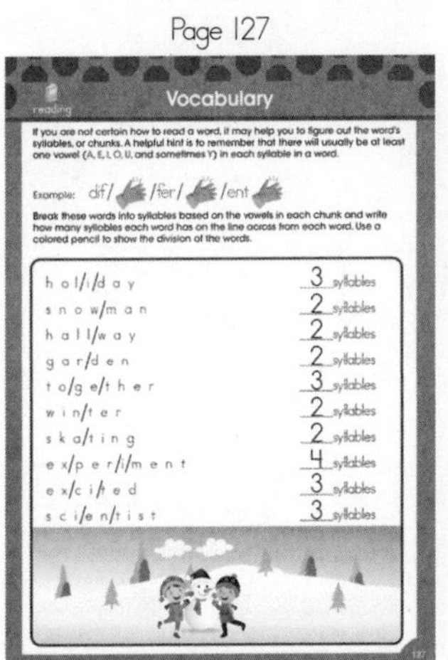
## Vocabulary

If you are not certain how to read a word, it may help you to figure out the word's syllables, or chunks.

| | |
|---|---|
| hol/i/day | 3 syllables |
| snow/man | 2 syllables |
| hall/way | 2 syllables |
| gar/den | 2 syllables |
| to/geth/er | 3 syllables |
| win/ter | 2 syllables |
| skat/ing | 2 syllables |
| ex/per/i/ment | 4 syllables |
| ex/cit/ed | 3 syllables |
| sci/en/tist | 3 syllables |

Page 128

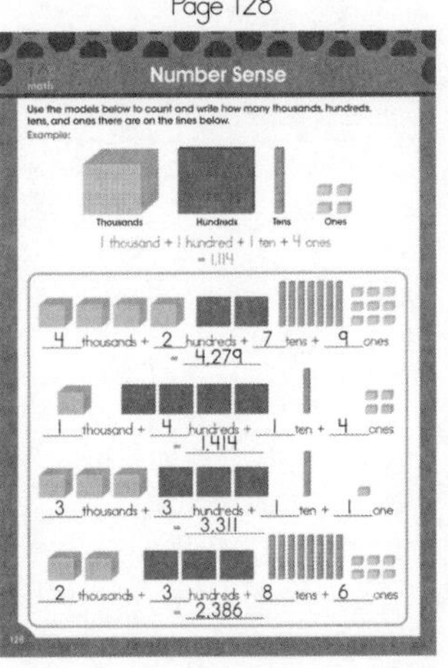
## Number Sense

Use the models below to count and write how many thousands, hundreds, tens, and ones there are on the lines below.

Example: 1 thousand + 1 hundred + 1 ten + 4 ones = 1,114

4 thousands + 2 hundreds + 7 tens + 9 ones = 4,279
1 thousand + 4 hundreds + 1 ten + 4 ones = 1,414
3 thousands + 3 hundreds + 1 ten + 1 one = 3,311
2 thousands + 3 hundreds + 8 tens + 6 ones = 2,386

Page 129

## Grammar

Homographs are words that have the same spelling, but different pronunciations and different meanings.

Example: bass and bass

I like the pretty bow in your hair. — A bow can be a sign of respect.
The wind is blowing very hard! — My brother will wind up the toy.
A dove landed on my windowsill! — Jason dove into the cold water.

Page 131

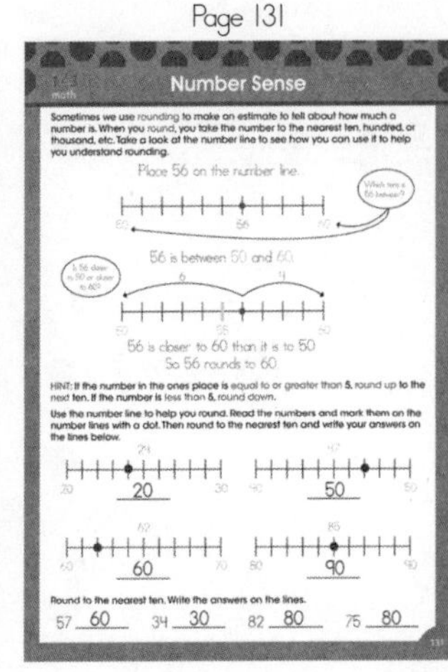
## Number Sense

Place 56 on the number line.
56 is between 50 and 60.
56 is closer to 60 than it is to 50. So 56 rounds to 60.

24 → 20; 47 → 50; 62 → 60; 85 → 90

Round to the nearest ten. Write the answers on the lines.

57 60 — 34 30 — 82 80 — 75 80

Page 132

## Grammar

Homonyms are words that have the same pronunciation and the same spelling but have different meanings.

Example: right and right

I wrote a letter to my best friend. — "I" is a word and a letter of the alphabet.
A palm tree can grow very tall. — I have ten cents in my palm.
My dad will park our car. — I love to play at the park.

Page 133

## Reading Comprehension

Follow the directions below to complete the neighborhood map.

1. Draw an American flag on a pole in front of the post office.
2. Draw your house in the southeast corner of the map.
3. Draw two children beside the school.
4. Draw a fire truck inside of the fire station.
5. Draw a car on Main Street driving toward the gas station.
6. Draw a librarian at the library holding a book.
7. Draw yourself on Orange Street near your house.

Page 134

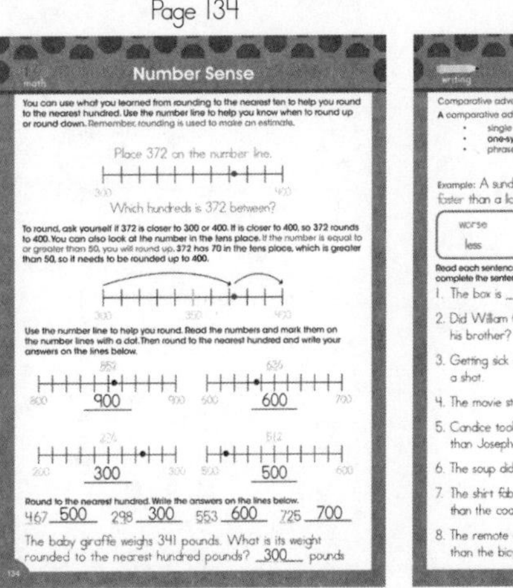
## Number Sense

Place 372 on the number line.
Which hundreds is 372 between?

889 → 900; 635 → 600; 275 → 300; 512 → 500

Round to the nearest hundred. Write the answers on the lines below.

467 500 — 298 300 — 553 600 — 725 700

The baby giraffe weighs 341 pounds. What is its weight rounded to the nearest hundred pounds? 300 pounds

Page 135

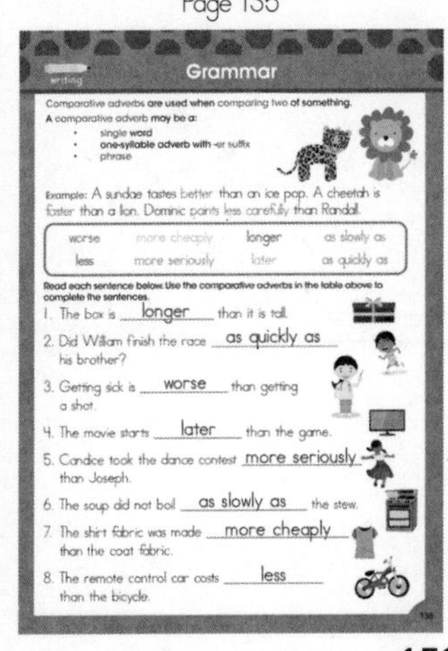
## Grammar

Comparative adverbs are used when comparing two of something.

Example: A sundae tastes better than an ice pop. A cheetah is faster than a lion. Dominic paints less carefully than Randall.

1. The box is longer than it is tall.
2. Did William finish the race as quickly as his brother?
3. Getting sick is worse than getting a shot.
4. The movie starts later than the game.
5. Candice took the dance contest more seriously than Joseph.
6. The soup did not boil as slowly as the stew.
7. The shirt fabric was made more cheaply than the coat fabric.
8. The remote control car costs less than the bicycle.

Page 138

## Level 10 Grade 3 Foundations

### Addition and Subtraction

You can use place value to help you add multi-digit numbers when you need to regroup.

Example: 256 + 538 = 200 + 50 + 6
500 + 30 + 8
700 + 80 + 14 = 794

Solve the equations below by using the place-value strategy and write the answers on the lines.

126 + 147 =
100 + 20 + 6
100 + 40 + 7
200 + 60 + 13 = 273

245 + 537 =
200 + 40 + 5
500 + 30 + 7
700 + 70 + 12 = 782

708 + 213 =
700 + 0 + 8
200 + 10 + 3
900 + 10 + 11 = 921

279 + 610 =
200 + 70 + 9
600 + 10 + 0
800 + 80 + 9 = 889

324 + 437 =
300 + 20 + 4
400 + 30 + 7
700 + 50 + 11 = 761

436 + 355 =
400 + 30 + 6
300 + 50 + 5
700 + 80 + 11 = 791

Solve the word problem by using the place-value strategy and write the equation and the sum in the box.

Alison is having a big party! She has 178 red party hats and 312 blue party hats. How many hats does Alison have for her party?

100 + 70 + 8
300 + 10 + 2
400 + 80 + 10 = 490

Page 139

### Addition and Subtraction

Adding hundreds, tens, and ones sometimes involves regrouping. If the numbers in a column add up to more than 9, you need to regroup to the next higher place value.

Practice adding and subtracting three-digit numbers. Write the answers in the boxes below.

| | Hundreds | Tens | Ones |
|---|---|---|---|
| | 3 | 2 | 1 |
| + | 4 | 3 | 7 |
| | 7 | 5 | 8 |

| | Hundreds | Tens | Ones |
|---|---|---|---|
| | 4 | 2 | 6 |
| − | 3 | 1 | 3 |
| | 1 | 1 | 3 |

| | Hundreds | Tens | Ones |
|---|---|---|---|
| | 7 | 0 | 3 |
| + | 1 | 1 | 3 |
| | 8 | 1 | 6 |

| | Hundreds | Tens | Ones |
|---|---|---|---|
| | 7 | 1 | 4 |
| − | 5 | 1 | 3 |
| | 2 | 0 | 1 |

| | Hundreds | Tens | Ones |
|---|---|---|---|
| | 2 | 9 | 9 |
| − | 1 | 0 | 7 |
| | 1 | 9 | 2 |

| | Hundreds | Tens | Ones |
|---|---|---|---|
| | 4 | 6 | 2 |
| + | 3 | 1 | 6 |
| | 7 | 7 | 8 |

| | Hundreds | Tens | Ones |
|---|---|---|---|
| | 6 | 3 | 7 |
| − | 5 | 2 | 2 |
| | 1 | 1 | 5 |

| | Hundreds | Tens | Ones |
|---|---|---|---|
| | 4 | 3 | 6 |
| + | 2 | 6 | 2 |
| | 6 | 9 | 8 |

| | Hundreds | Tens | Ones |
|---|---|---|---|
| | 5 | 5 | 3 |
| − | 4 | 3 | 2 |
| | 1 | 2 | 1 |

Answer the number sense questions and write your answers on the lines.

What number is in the tens place of the number 274? 7
What number is in the ones place of the number 680? 0
What number is in the hundreds place of the number 175? 1
How many tens are in the number 369? 6

Page 140

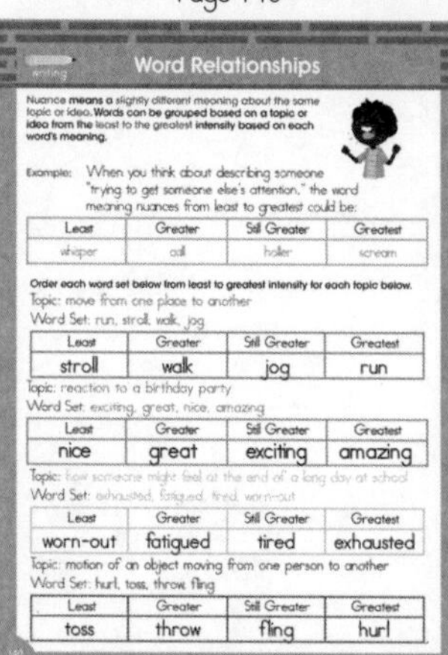

Page 141

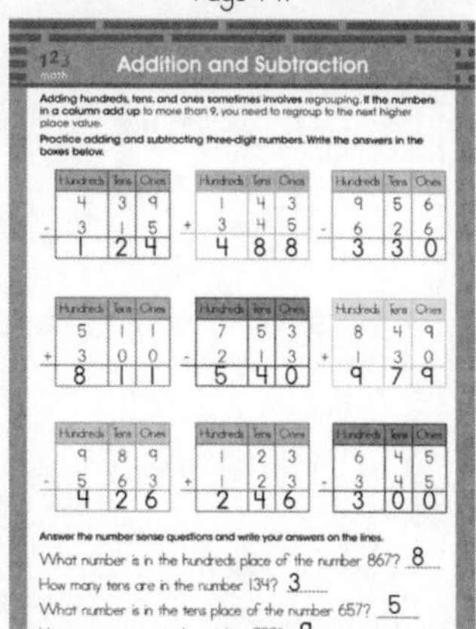

Page 142

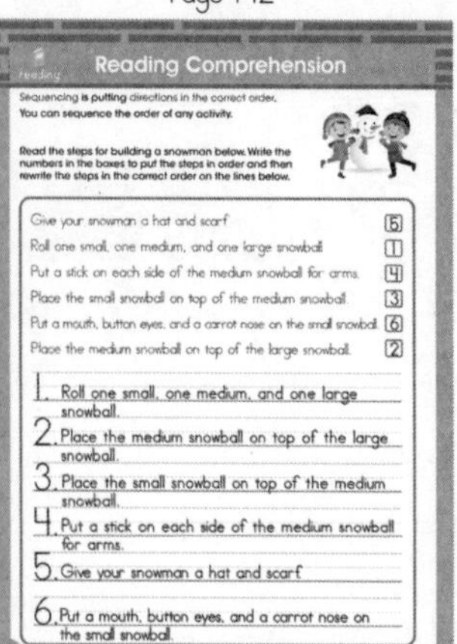

Page 143

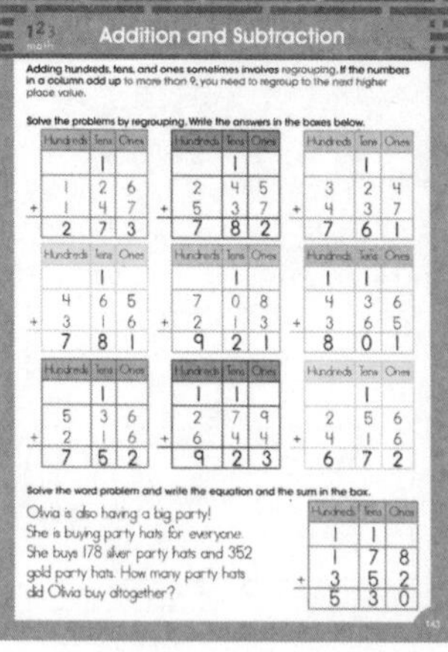

Page 144

Page 145

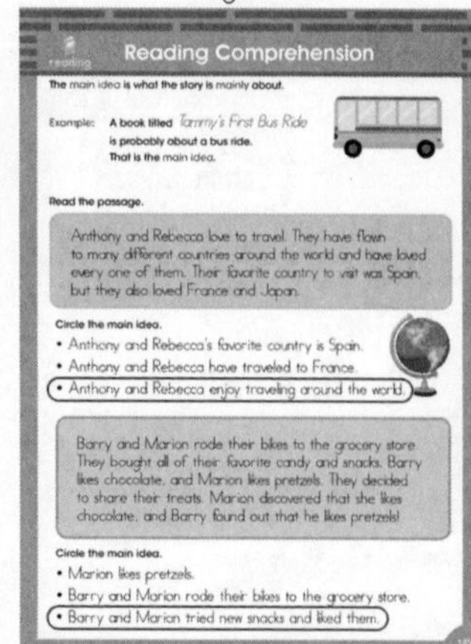

Page 146

Page 147

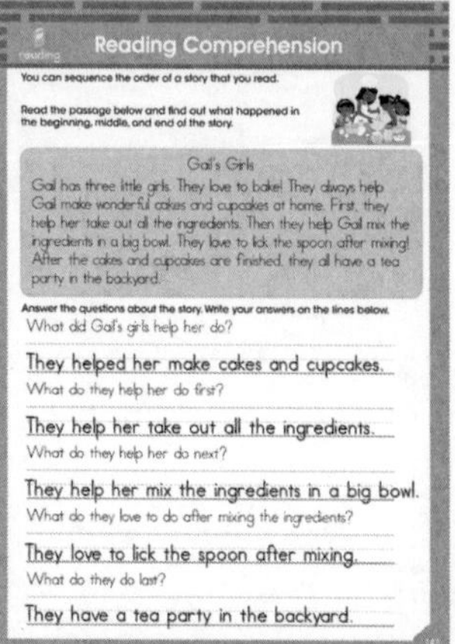

Page 148

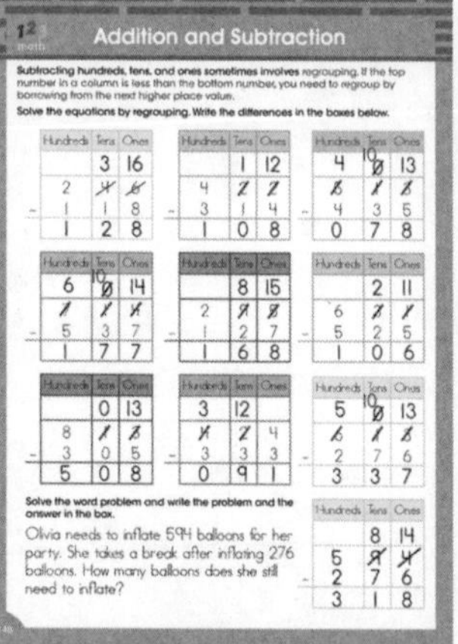

Page 149

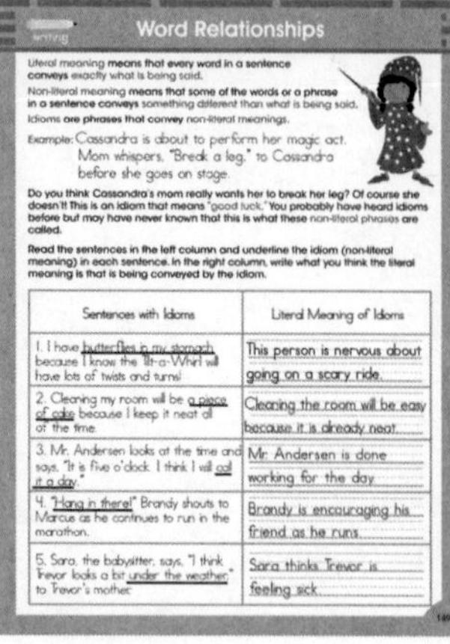

Page 150

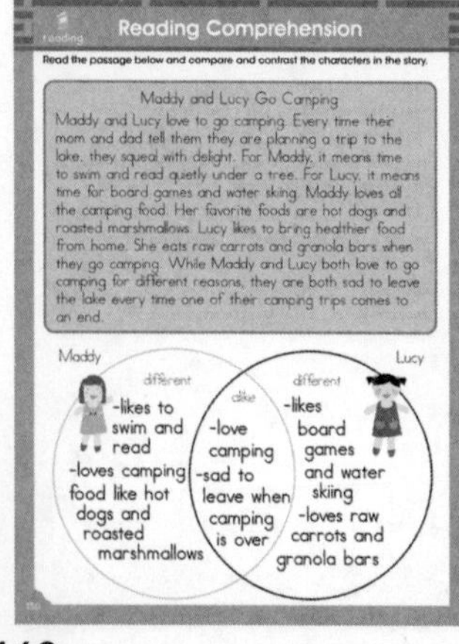

Page 151

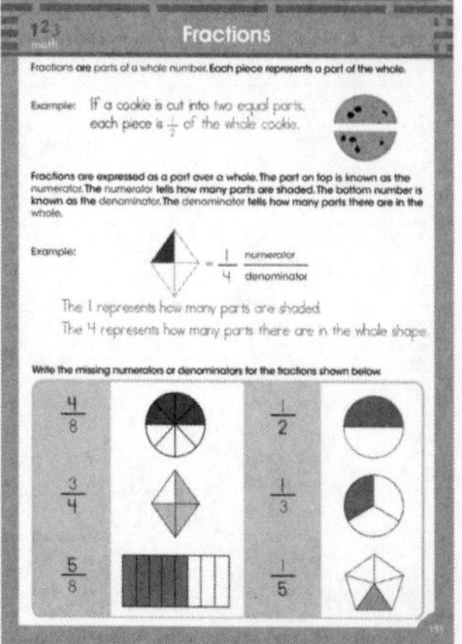

Page 152

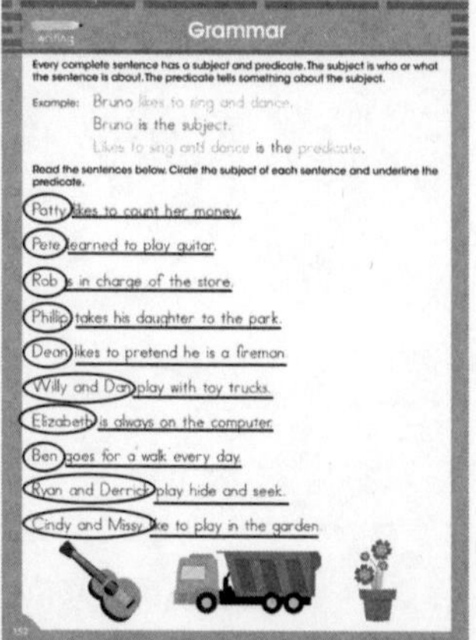